Human Capital Analytics

Measuring and Improving Learning and Talent Impact

Human Capital Analytics

Measuring and Improving Learning and Talent Impact

By Kent Barnett & Jeffrey Berk

Printed in the United States of America.

ISBN 10: 1-59571-186-4
ISBN 13: 978-1-59571-186-1
Library of Congress Control Number: 2007925481

Word Association Publishers
205 Fifth Avenue
Tarentum, Pennsylvania 15084
www.wordassociation.com
1-800-827-7903
fax: 724-226-3974

Contents

I. Why Analyze Human Capital Impact?. 4

II. Business Case for Measurement 5

III. Identifying Human Capital Processes 10

IV. Current Trends in Learning Measurement 30

V. Human Capital Contribution Model™. 53

    Business Needs Analysis 62

    Performance Analysis. 69

    Business Results Analysis. 85

    ROI Analysis. 105

    Profit Impact Analysis. 119

VI. Overview of Learning Analytics and Measurement Models 124

VII. Presenting a Measurement Method That Is Practical and Scalable 148

VIII. Valuation Models for Deriving Impact, Results, and ROI. 164

IX. Key Performance Indicators and Dashboards 210

X. Change Management in Analytics. 239

XI. Outsourcing Analytics Components. 244

XII. Best Practices in Learning Analytics. 249

Footnotes: 265

I. Why Analyze Human Capital Impact?

The old adage "what gets measured gets done" certainly applies to the world of human capital investment. Research shows that measuring the impact of learning and development programs creates significant shareholder value.

Dr. Gary Becker's Nobel-Prize-winning work on human capital proves that well-designed employee education programs have a bigger impact on future earnings than any other investment. It also proves that learning and development programs that are not measured usually result in significantly lower productivity than those that are measured.

Why don't most organizations measure learning and talent impact? Our research shows two primary reasons why organizations historically have not measured learning impact:

1) Data collection and reporting. Prior to the advent of the Internet, collecting and reporting impact related to data was costly. Web-based evaluation and analysis technologies such as Metrics That Matter provide robust and low-cost solutions to this problem.

2) Proven methodologies. Prior to Dr. Becker's work and Dr. Jack Phillips's ground-breaking ROI Process, the only accepted methodology for measuring impact was statistical analysis.

Now both academia and major corporations accept the Phillips ROI Process as a cost-effective way to measure learning impact.

Caterpillar University and Defense Acquisition University are among the award-winning corporate universities that have dispelled the myth that you cannot measure learning impact. Both organizations, led by a former chief economist, Dave Vance, and a retired general, Frank Anderson, respectively, have taken a data-driven approach to measuring impact. We have had the pleasure of working with both organizations and seeing firsthand how measurement can drive shareholder and taxpayer value.

II. Business Case for Measurement

In order to invest energy in any endeavor it has to mean something. It must be significant to the individual or organization. Without commitment and ownership, initiatives fade away like a flavor of the month. This chapter will present a compelling argument for measuring learning investments by understanding the reasons why metrics are a priority in today's business environment.

Not so long ago we heard from a large logistics company, "Our annual IT training budget depends on two things: business profitability and the success we have in making the case that training is essential for the business." The company was struggling with justification for technology training and was searching for compelling data to convince their management that in profitable and unprofitable times, their learning programs must survive. The business case for this organization was to prove how *essential* learning was to the *organization*.

A welding company in Europe provides another example. They stated, "We are very interested in measuring the ROI of training and certification, but we don't know of a feasible method for doing this." Management at this company wanted to take a financial approach to validating learning investments just as they did with any other investment within the firm (marketing, property, plant, and equipment). The business case in this situation was ROI in a classic financial sense. However, the learning organization needed to do this in a *feasible* manner. They did not have the resources (money, time, people) to do large-scale measurement with precision. They needed their business case for ROI to be met through practical approaches that had scalability throughout their learning organization.

To further validate the growing need for learning measurement within a customer, partner, or employee education setting, one need only look to the growing research reports that continue to rank this issue as a top challenge for the learning and development (L&D) industry. For example *T&D* magazine, the publication of the American Society of Training & Development (ASTD), released research in

January and February of 2006 that had the following findings:

> #1 Challenge of L&D Organizations: Proving value / ROI of Training
> #1 Challenge of Chief Learning Officers: Communicating and Measuring Results

What these research findings suggest is that issues like e-Learning, employee engagement, talent management, LMS implementations, or leadership programs are not what trouble those in learning the most. It is the relentless request (or demand in some cases) to validate or justify what has been done and to communicate that in a timely and meaningful way to those who make future budget decisions.

What this research suggests is that a twenty-first-century worker lives in an era of accountability to which nobody is immune. A marketing person who wants to run an ad on Super bowl Sunday better make sure there is analysis behind it to prove the juice was worth the squeeze.

This is the same for consultants who are re-engineering business processes. If money is to be allocated to produce more efficient processes, there needs to be some quantification of the effort and some linkage to the business results that it will ultimately affect. To throw millions of dollars at an initiative with no forecast of the future state and no follow-up to ensure that the desired state was met is not consistent with accountability.

In not-for-profit organizations accountability is referred to as stewardship. Being a good steward of donations within charitable organizations has become a high priority. Within the L&D organizations of not-for-profits we have seen intensified pressure to prove that the budget for learning is being used appropriately so that the board of directors can ensure proper stewardship of funds placed in their trust. For example, a not-for-profit that assists organizations that employ the severely handicapped was challenged by their board to provide evidence of learning impact beyond the number of people who accessed e-Learning, participated in a book club, or took an instructor-led workshop.

This board demanded to understand whether executives who attended the learning programs gained value from it. Although one popular program had a 98% satisfaction rate and 80% of participants recommended it to others that was not enough. Results-driven data was needed. One executive who attended the program reduced turnover from 125% to 85% within her organization as a result of the concepts applied from the program. Another executive doubled the size of a customer contract (a $250,000 increase) because he utilized the tools from the program. Accountability was the Kool-Aid that this board wanted to drink.

Accountability is being a good steward. It is, as Gary Logsdon of Air Products would say, "minding our store." It means that management was provided with appropriate, quantifiable evidence to validate that the continued investments in L&D are good for the organization. Others would say measurement is needed to validate, not justify. Tom Hilgart, Vice President of Learning and Knowledge Sharing for CNA Insurance, says just that. He believes that senior management is convinced of learning's strategic value and would not cut that investment cold- turkey. But, as the owner of that function, Tom feels a necessary responsibility to validate what they know is strategic through quantified metrics. Justification in Tom's eyes is the negative side of it where the executives never felt there was value. Validation in Tom's eyes is very different because management knows there is value; the metrics help to reinforce that belief.

Accountability has never been more glaring than in the case of the GAO. Up until 2004, the GAO was the acronym for "General Accounting Office." In 2004, the name was changed to "Government Accountability Office." It was part of their Human Capital Reform Act of 2004. They cited the need to no longer simply count dollars spent but to ensure that how and where it was spent was appropriate — the change and the PR that announced it showed how serious they were about this change — that's accountability.

So a significant business case is one of accountability. Whether it be minding the store, justification, validation, stewardship, or plain old accountability, it exists in every aspect of business where we do more with less. It is also necessary in today's microscopic world. Every decision might result in bad PR or an organizational risk. Post Enron, executives need to be very careful in how they allocate resources for fear of being labeled irresponsible or asleep at the wheel.

The economic argument for measuring learning and talent impact is overwhelming. According to IDC, a typical Fortune 500 company or government agency invests approximately 2% of their revenue in L&D. If half is wasted, that means organizations, on average, waste 1% of revenue. An organization that has $5 billion in revenue is probably wasting $50 million per year. In our example, reducing waste by only 10% will improve earnings by $500,000.

It is for the above reasons that metrics matter. Learning and development is a significant expense for most organizations. If you're not an accountant, please understand that this large number is material and anything material makes accountants nervous. L&D operations can increase comfort and confidence by providing a continual flow of measurement data to the stakeholders. The remainder of this book will explain how to do it. We hope you read on!

III. Identifying Human Capital Processes

Although this book will outline in detail steps toward measuring a major contributor to a high performing workforce, learning and development, it is also important to take a step back and present how all human capital and talent management processes need better measurement. There are several significant benefits associated with the measurement of human capital managed processes. The most significant include a series of strategic and tactical benefits:

Strategic:
• Catalyst for creating the high performance workforce that will increase productivity, quality and customer satisfaction while decreasing employee turnover, business risk, and cycle time

• Significant driver of financial results: increased revenue and decreased costs

• Key contributor to wealth creation / stakeholder value: market value exceeding book value

Tactical:
• Quickly identify gaps that exist in the management of the human capital process

• Ensure the management of the human capital process is functioning as designed

• Steer limited resources (financial, physical, human) toward improving the human capital process that needs it the most

• Improve outcome results of human capital processes (ex. analyzing exit interview data at a tactical and strategic level can result in less employee turnover and better recruiting processes)

In general, human capital processes should be reviewed on a continuous basis to ensure they are functioning as designed to achieve the aforementioned benefits. There are six primary drivers of process change that may cause human capital processes to become out of alignment. Through appropriate diagnostics and continuous measurement these six drivers of change can and will detect problems and mitigate their effects in a timely manner.

1. People Changes: Processes that have heavy turnover or turnover of key personnel or personnel no longer qualified for the skill or competency demanded of the role are at risk.

2. Process Changes: Processes that have organizational structure change or changes to the inputs that feed them, the activities (i.e. policies and procedures) within them or the outputs that produce are at risk.

3. Technology Changes: Processes that have changes to information technology systems are at risk.

4. Culture/Leadership Changes: Processes that have changes in the senior or executive management levels are at risk.

5. Measurement Changes: Processes that change the way the team or individual is measured in terms of performance are at risk.

6. External Changes: Changes outside of the process or organization including economic, political, regulatory, and competitive change are at risk.

Human Capital Analytics Defined
Human Capital Analytics is the process of measuring human capital processes from recruitment to retirement and all people management processes in between.

This definition means that Human Capital Analytics measures, not manages. It quantifies gaps in the management of existing processes to more precisely identify opportunities for improvement where limited financial, physical and human resources exist for improvement.

An example of this is the learning and development process, a component of the overall human capital process. A learning management system manages the day-to-day learning operation. Examples include registering attendees or tracking completions. A learning analytics system measures the outcomes of the day-to-day learning operation such as the effectiveness of the learning the attendees received or the impact the learning had on the job. By performing practical measurement the learning and development organization can identify what curricula are least effective and target their resources toward improving those versus others. Those improvements are then built back into the management process of learning and development.

Human Capital Process Classification Scheme
In 1992 several founding members of the American
Productivity and Quality Center's International
Benchmarking Clearinghouse created a Universal
Process Classification Scheme comprised of 13 core
business processes and over 100 sub-processes that
apply to almost any business regardless of
geography, size, or industry. Within the framework
is one titled Develop and Manage Human Resources.

Rather than create a new classification scheme, it is a
best practice to leverage industry accepted models
such as the Universal Process Classification Scheme.
As such KnowledgeAdvisors has adapted this scheme
in the creation of the Human Capital Process
Classification Scheme.

1. Manage Deployment of Personnel
a. Forecast Workforce Requirements
b. Recruit, Select, and Hire
c. Succession Planning
d. International Assignment
e. Mobile Workforce
f. Employee Turnover

2. Manage Competencies and Performance
a. Competency Management
b. Performance Appraisal

3. Develop and Train Employees
a. New Hire / On-boarding
b. Learning and Development

c. Coaching and Mentoring
d. Leadership Development
e. Knowledge Management

4. Motivate and Retain Employees
a. Compensation and Benefits
b. Employee Satisfaction
c. Employee Engagement
d. Work/Life Balance
e. Workforce Diversity

The aforementioned 4 processes and related 18 sub-processes allow all organizations, regardless of geography, size or industry, to assess the completeness of their human capital management. It is from this mutually exclusive/collectively exhaustive framework that allows KnowledgeAdvisors to measure human capital managed processes.

Human Capital Measurement Process Flow
The illustration below highlights the flow in maximizing human capital from business strategy to wealth creation.

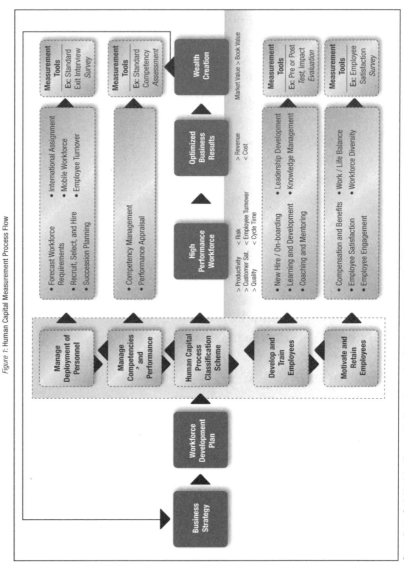

Figure 1: Human Capital Measurement Process Flow

Source: Human Capital Analytics: Measuring the People Process From Recruitment to Retirement, KnowledgeAdvisors

The process begins with a human resource executive understanding the business strategy. This is the driver of all future decisions. It ensures from the beginning that any human capital decisions will be aligned with the organizational business strategy.

After reviewing the business strategy, the human resource executive should build a workforce development plan. The plan should achieve the strategic business goals through the desired workforce.

The workforce must then be calibrated to achieve the workforce development plan. This is done through four major enablers who formulate the previously discussed Human Capital Process Classification Scheme: Manage Deployment of Personnel, Manage Competencies and Performance, Develop and Train Employees and Motivate and Retain Employees. There are sub-processes beneath these four major enablers and for each there are measurement tools in the form of templates, standards and technology to measure these processes to ensure they are successfully managed and achieving their intended purpose.

The direct results of solid human capital measurement are effectively managed processes that yield a high performance workforce. This is a workforce that has the following attributes when measured:
Increased Productivity
Increased Quality

Increased Customer Satisfaction
Decreased Risk
Decreased Employee Turnover
Decreased Cycle Time

If these metrics are moving in the right direction the organization has achieved optimized business results. The most significant results tie to the financial statement, primarily the income statement. If measured the revenues have increased and the costs have decreased yielding higher margins.

The results of healthy financial performance produce the ultimate effect of human capital value: wealth creation. Wealth creation is increased stakeholder value. Stakeholders include the following:

Taxpayers (for public sector organizations)
Shareholders (for corporations)
Employees
Partners

The most obvious example is when the market value of a company exceeds its book value. This is the marketplace's approval of successfully managed organizations, including human capital processes.

There is documented evidence that publicly traded organizations that optimally manage human capital processes will yield higher stock prices. In the published study <u>The Impact of U.S. Firms Investments in Human Capital on Stock Prices.</u> This research found a "super normal" return to a firm's investment in human capital and in particular a firm's training investments. The study cites quantifiable differences in the high performing workforce results cited above (productivity, quality, customer satisfaction, employee retention) and to financial results (sales). In addition the findings positively correlate the stock price of those organizations that made investments in human capital.

Human Capital Measurement Model & Tools
Measurement models and tools must support the Human Capital Process Classification Scheme. The models and tools allow for theory to be brought to reality and allow ideas to be brought to action.

First let's discuss the model. Measurement is organized around data. There must be a model to administer for measurement to ensure it will function as designed. The main areas of emphasis for the measurement model are as follows:

1. Collection
2. Storage
3. Processing
4. Reporting
5. Analysis
6. Improvement

The key here is to recognize that some of these steps are administrative and 'ready the data' and do not add value. Those steps are collection, storage, processing, and reporting. No decisions have been made yet until one analyzes the data and makes improvements. The goal therefore in human capital analytics is to have the right tools to streamline the administrative aspects of measurement. Tools will be discussed shortly.

Collection of data is an essential first step. Data may be gathered through sources such as spreadsheets, databases, and feeder systems like an HRIS, LMS, or ERP. Further one can use evaluation systems, surveys, assessments, interviews, and focus groups as data inputs.

Storage of data is important as well. The goal is to store the human capital metrics in a centralized database. This is important in the processing power of the data originating from one source. It also mitigates risk of processing the wrong 'version' of data if it resides in multiple sources. Further, centralization of data is important in ensuring that the users of the information can begin to see the inter-relationships in the metrics not only within a process or sub-process in the Human Capital Process Classification Scheme but also between processes in the framework.

Processing of data can be time consuming and cumbersome. It is important to use some sophistication especially with large amounts of data. Online analytical processing (OLAP) tools allow for better "slicing and dicing" of data in a user friendly manner. The ability to quickly aggregate and drill down into the data is equally important.

Reporting of data should be self sufficient. It should allow users to generate their own custom reports for their own analysis. Standard reporting templates should be automated and online to allow for this self sufficiency.

Analysis of data should focus in three primary areas: 1) trends showcasing how the metrics are directionally moving, 2) goals to understand if the metrics are reaching desired levels of performance, and 3) benchmarks to glean insights against relevant points of internal or external reference. Improvements should be made in a timely manner. Solid analysis will show the largest gaps in performance to make pinpointing improvement opportunities clear. Improvements should be classified into short, intermediate and long term improvements and should use classifications such as cost/benefit, risk, strategic vs. tactical in the thought process.

The tools that should be used throughout measurement will in no doubt be specific to the process within the framework. However a common theme should exist across them all. The three primary tools to which customized tools are created are the following:

1.   Templates
2.   Standards
3.   Technology

Templates are structured tools that allow functional users assessing human capital processes with facilitated and consultative mechanisms to collect data. For example, a forecasting tool to determine the ROI on a leadership development program prior to program development can be determined through a well structured template.

Standards are critical to ensuring data is consistent and comparable. Anytime an evaluation, survey or assessment is used, the ability to start with a standard is important. Standards can exist in every human capital process in the process classification scheme noted above. For example if you desire to study employee turnover there may be a standard exit interview survey. This standard allows the organization to start with a credible starting point and add to it. Further it will likely have benchmarks surrounding it so there is a comparable element to it. Consistent data and comparable data through standards make the data more actionable for information decision making. Seek out standards when engaging in human capital analytics before building your own evaluations, tests, surveys, or assessments.

It is important to understand the uniqueness of each standard instrument:

Evaluation: This is a tool that measures the perception of a prior outcome. This is very common in learning and development. An end of class evaluation is done to determine the effectiveness and predicted impact of the learning in the eyes of the participants or their manager.

Test: This is a tool to more objectively measure knowledge or skill. This is common in learning and development and in competency management and certifications for workforce planning. A pre vs. post test may be used to measure increased in knowledge or skill.

Survey: This is a tool used to measure the respondent's opinion of a stated circumstance. This is common in many areas of human capital. Examples include employee satisfaction and exit interviews.

Assessments: This is a tool that is used to measure perception of knowledge, skills, competencies or desired outcomes. This is common in competency management whereby a competency assessment may ask employees to rank their competencies in areas such as business or financial acumen.

Technology is important to minimizing administration burdens. There are many inexpensive tools that exist that can collect any type of survey data. There are also tools that are empty warehouses waiting to be filled with data from feeder systems. The key is to have the right technology that can compliment your human capital analytic business needs. Good technologies will provide for data collection that leverages standards when using evaluations, surveys, or assessments. It will also have templates for manual or automated data feeds from feeder systems such as Access databases, Excel files,

HRIS systems, ERP systems or an LMS system. In addition, it allows the functional user performing basic and advanced human capital analytics to do so in a self-sufficient manner. This is commonly done through user friendly interfaces to query the data not only by the attributes of the human capital process but by the attributes of the human capital itself.

For example if we are measuring high employee turnover at a large retail environment we would start with a standard exit interview survey that can be collected across all stores. The data capture would be done via the Internet. The data is stored in a single repository. It can be queried or processed by items on the survey itself (reason for leaving, etc.) but also by the store location, the employee job level, the years of service etc. The data can be aggregated at the region, district and overall company levels to look at trends. It can also be compared against internal and external benchmarks, goals, and trends. Finally and most importantly, the analysis of such data reported in this manner is fed back into the employee turnover process AND complimentary processes such as the recruitment process to improve the management of them.

Risks Associated with Human Capital Measurement
There are risks associated with human capital measurement. These include the following:

• Data protection. This is a serious risk. Collecting data about human resource information can run into legal risk. A way to mitigate this risk is by ensuring any vendor working with you to do this has a safe harbor certification for human resource data. This can be found at http://www.export.gov/safeharbor/. This ensures that the policies and procedures of those working with you on human capital process improvement have had their policies and procedures reviewed by a third party to ensure they conform to international standards.

• Data security. This is slightly different but complimentary to data protection. This is looking closer at systems and physical security once done is collected. Organizations should ensure vendors working on human capital analytics have the following security safeguards:

    ☐ Physical security
    ☐ Network security
    ☐ Host quality control
    ☐ Application quality control
    ☐ Backup procedures
    ☐ Disaster recovery plans

• Customization/Configuration. Although the Human Capital Process Classification Scheme is meant to help organizations communicate and share best practices and benchmarks around human capital management, there also should be room for customization and configuration. Ensure that the human capital analytics partner you work with is able to understand your individual needs and customize or configure the measurement templates, standards, and technologies to those needs.

• Adaptability. Processes change as time changes. Human capital managed processes such as those in the Human Capital Process Classification Scheme should be reviewed on a regular basis to ensure they continue to function as designed and are not exposed to significant risk due to business climate changes. Being able to identify problems before they are a significant risk and adapt to them is a key to effective human resource analytics functions.

Action Steps to Start Effective Human Capital Measurement

In order to begin effective human capital measurement a readiness assessment of the processes outlined in the Human Capital Process Classification Scheme should be conducted. This readiness assessment is a 'mile wide –inch deep' view of these processes. The objective of the assessment is to understand where gaps and improvement opportunities lie. Once done a drill down into more detailed diagnostics to assess at the individual process level is done.

For example, if the readiness assessment reveals significant risk in the employee turnover process, a more detailed diagnostic could be done to understand that process better. If it is revealed from the process diagnostic that exit interview data is not being conducted in a consistent, timely and aggregate manner then a measurement that is put in place is a standard exit interview survey to help measure this function in a more effective manner. In this example the exit interview is the measurement mechanism that may stay in place and become a part of the process to ensure it is managed better, with reliable data for information decision making.

In summary the steps would be:

1. Conduct a high level, 'macro' diagnostic to review all processes in the Human Capital Process Classification Scheme and determine the specific processes with the largest gaps. In this case the diagnostic goes across the four enablers in the scheme: Manage Deployment of Personnel, Manage Competencies and Performance, Develop and Train Employees and Motivate and Retain Employees.

2. The next step is to conduct a more tactical diagnostic within a specific sub-process in one or more enabling processes. In the example above one would have looked at the Manage Deployment of Personnel then the Employee Turnover process to drill into the exit interview measurement.

3. The process is injected with measurement into it. This will help in managing it better. The standard exit interview that is aggregated across the company would be the example.

4. As measures help manage improvements can be made to the process and complimentary processes. In the example the exit interview data analysis can help the recruit, select and hire process by feeding it with

information on the type of people that typically leave the organization.

The diagram below illustrates the flow of these actions steps:

Figure 2: Action Steps for Effective Human Capital Measurement

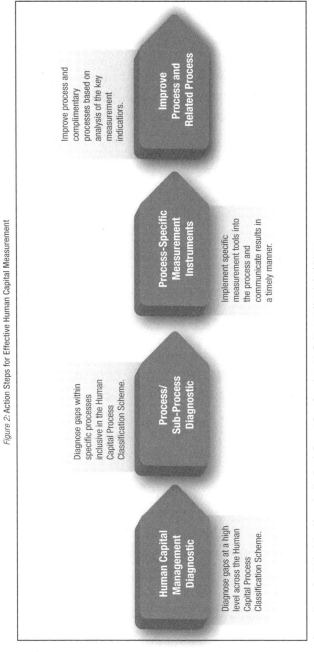

Source: Human Capital Analytics: Measuring the People Process From Recruitment to Retirement, KnowledgeAdvisors

IV. Current Trends in Learning Measurement

Before we dive into the details about human capital measurement, a nice segue from business case to methodology is to understand the research that supports both.

Numerous research studies have been done recently within the L&D industry to understanding what should be measured, why it needs to be measured, how it should be measured, and when to measure it. This chapter will present the highlights of some of this research.

Learning metrics are no longer a "nice to have" or just for the strategic, visible, or costly programs. Credible metrics are needed to represent the entire L&D budget and the subsets of it. In addition, the research suggests the following helpful hints for making analytics successful in large, complicated, multinational learning environments:

1. Automate the activities underneath data collection, processing, storage, and reporting.
2. Leverage forecasts and predictive indicators to make decisions before and during a learning program, not just after it is finished — and the cost is sunk.
3. Focus on templates and standards for comparable and consistent data.

4. Build a strategy and set of processes that are practical and can scale across all learning interventions.
5. Create evaluation tools that provide indicators of the following learning levels to help ensure a balanced focus in metrics:
   a. Learner satisfaction
   b. Learning effectiveness
   c. Job impact
   d. Linkage to business results
   e. Return on investment
6. Derive a dashboard of key macro drivers and micro indicators to monitor the health of the L&D organization as well as the larger organization to which the L&D belongs.

All of the above will be targeted for discussion later in this book. Let's see what the research says, though, about how well we're doing in getting to these best practices.

Our first research finding is illustrated in Figure 3. This chart, from Bersin & Associates, asked respondents the first tough question around metrics: "Are you spending enough on training measurement?" The answer overwhelmingly was no. In fact, 82% of the organizations studied felt they needed to spend more or much more on this endeavor. A benchmark that may be helpful is that organizations should spend 3% to 7% of their L&D budget on measurement of the other 93% to 97% of it. Yet we consistently see no formal budget line item for this important task.

Think about a supply chain in contrast to learning. A supply chain spends significant resources in the Q&A process. The cost of errors and the reputation risk of recalls and returns is too high for them not to do this. Scrap is something that manufacturing concerns try to prevent through good controls and solid metrics. L&D can gain creative insight from this by building in the appropriate budget for its metrics process. Budget legitimizes the effort and nothing will get done without it.

Figure 3: Monies Spent on Training Measurement

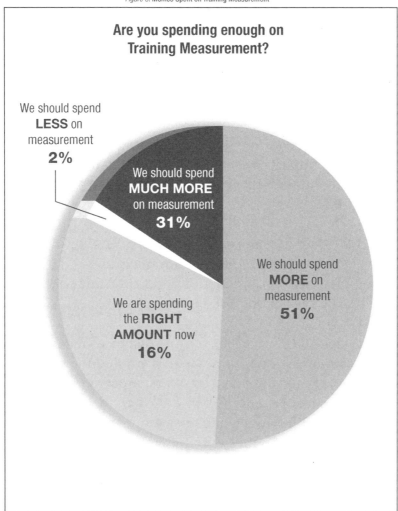

Figure 3: Monies Spent on Training Measurement

Are you spending enough on Training Measurement?

We should spend **LESS** on measurement **2%**

We should spend **MUCH MORE** on measurement **31%**

We should spend **MORE** on measurement **51%**

We are spending the **RIGHT AMOUNT** now **16%**

Source: Bersin & Associates

Figures 4, 5, and 6 illustrate what constitutes a desirable measurement outcome, what is actually being measured, and how much progress (or lack thereof) we've made in narrowing these gaps.

Desired measures by management include evidence of job impact, a demonstrable link between learning and actual business results, or indicators of how learning impacts business results. Even manager satisfaction with the learning is highly ranked. See Figure 4.

Yet typically it is the easier and less meaningful items that get measured. Information regarding completions, enrollments, and Level I smile sheets are typically measured. See Figure 5.

Between 2004 and 2006, in some instances the L&D industry digressed from where it wanted to be. More organizations measured business impact, actual business results, and ROI in 2004 than in 2006. Perhaps with budget cuts, measurement took a back seat to other activities within L&D. However, accountability has become stronger since 2004. This only illustrates that the L&D focus is not becoming aligned with the business but moving further from it.

Figure 4: Desirable Learning Metrics

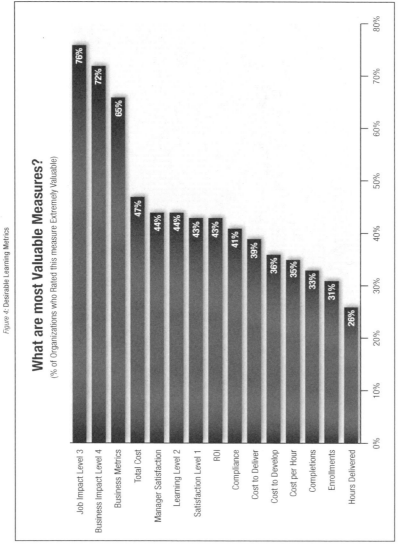

What are most Valuable Measures?
(% of Organizations who Rated this measure Extremely Valuable)

Job Impact Level 3	76%
Business Impact Level 4	72%
Business Metrics	65%
Total Cost	47%
Manager Satisfaction	44%
Learning Level 2	44%
Satisfaction Level 1	43%
ROI	43%
Compliance	41%
Cost to Deliver	39%
Cost to Develop	36%
Cost per Hour	35%
Completions	33%
Enrollments	31%
Hours Delivered	26%

Source: Bersin & Associates

Figure 5: Actual Learning Metrics

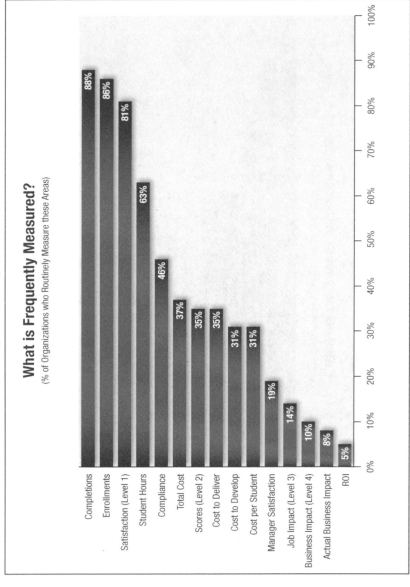

What is Frequently Measured?
(% of Organizations who Routinely Measure these Areas)

Source: Bersin & Associates

Figure 6: Measurement Trends

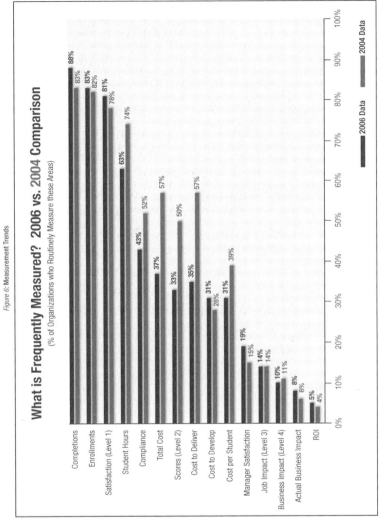

What is Frequently Measured? 2006 vs. 2004 Comparison

(% of Organizations who Routinely Measure these Areas)

■ 2006 Data   ■ 2004 Data

Category	2006	2004
Completions	88%	83%
Enrollments	83%	82%
Satisfaction (Level 1)	81%	78%
Student Hours	63%	74%
Compliance	43%	52%
Total Cost	37%	57%
Scores (Level 2)	33%	50%
Cost to Deliver	35%	57%
Cost to Develop	31%	28%
Cost per Student	31%	39%
Manager Satisfaction	19%	15%
Job Impact (Level 3)	14%	14%
Business Impact (Level 4)	10%	11%
Actual Business Impact	8%	6%
ROI	5%	4%

Source: Bersin & Associates

So let's understand where the limited resources that are spent on measurement are going. If they result in not measuring the right things, why?

In Figure 7 we can see where the limited money, time, and people that go into learning measurement are being dispersed. This figure tells us that 81% of resources flow into administrative, non-value-added tasks of measurement that are "readying" the data for analysis tasks. We say this because no decision on the data has yet been made while doing collection, aggregation, filtering, and reporting. A key lesson to be learned from this chart is to streamline, automate, and create standards and templates for the administrative tasks of measurement so that more resources can be spent analyzing data for information decision making.

Figure 7. Resource Allocation for Measurement

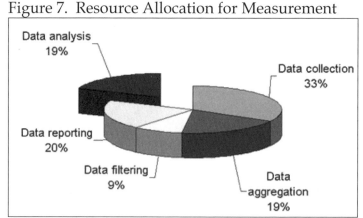

Source: KnowledgeAdvisors, Learning Analytics Best Practices Research Study, 2004

According to another research finding, the majority of L&D organizations don't report a consistent set of key performance indicators. Management that appears to be ever changing as well as highly customized or tactical program-level metrics don't lend themselves to painting a clear picture of whether or not the overall L&D group is moving in the right direction and is aligned with the business strategy. See Figure 8. Nearly two thirds of organizations don't track a common set of key performance indicators for learning.

Figure 8. L&D Existence of Key Performance Indicators

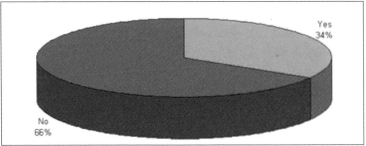

Source: KnowledgeAdvisors, Learning Analytics Best Practices Research Study, 2004

The most compelling research is presented in Figure 9. The L&D organizations interviewed seemed to have an unwritten rule that unless a number is precise and statistically valid it has no value and is therefore not measured. However, think about other aspects of your organization. They use metrics to validate a gut instinct and make future decisions. The data they use is more timely than precise. In fact, some might say the data is "roughly reasonable."

Think about a sales organization, for example. A sales manager does not wait until the audited, exact sales figures are completed before reporting them to senior management. In fact, sales managers have forecasts for sales at least a year in advance. They leverage reasonable indicators of product launches, economic indicators, political factors, historical trends, and other upcoming events to predict sales. They apply an adjustment factor to account for imprecision in the analysis and use the final forecasts for goal setting and performance measurement.

However, L&D organizations tend to hide behind the "impossibility of linking learning to results" and the notion that because it cannot be precise it won't be done. A sales manager who said that to management would not be the sales manager very long. In a world of business, data is more powerful if more timely than more precise. Most L&D managers who run commercial learning programs or employee education programs must realize this to be successful in measurement. It's okay to have reasonable, timely data. Unless you are in an academic environment doing research, you have the constraints of making decisions in a timely manner. Recognize this and adapt your measurement models to it, just as sales has done for years.

The aforementioned is supported by Figure 9. This figure shows that there are three approaches to metric precision:
   1. Highly precise, statistically accurate measurements

2. Word-of-mouth anecdotal statements
3. Reasonable quantitative and qualitative data

The first approach is the best. No debate about it. Unfortunately it is the most costly and time-consuming. The metrics may not be delivered for months or years. The program has run multiple times and after that it doesn't matter any more. It is not practical to take this approach all the time because the rule of timeliness of data is not met.

The second approach can be timely, but just asking a few people their opinions may not yield an accurate representation of the population and any form of quantifiable data.

The third approach wins out. Reasonable data of a qualitative and quantitative nature can be collected in a timely manner. It is credible if it is a solid representation of the population and builds in adjustment factors for imprecision in the data. That's why the overwhelming majority of consumers of learning measurement data prefer it to the other two methods.

If you're building a measurement strategy and process, the concept of "roughly reasonable" is a critical first step. You don't want to put a highly precise process in place that cannot scale throughout your business. You'll be on the defensive — and that's not a good position to be in.

A quick story to illustrate the point. A major cable company had a leadership program. It was very visible. The L&D manager spent nine months compiling precise data on the effects of the program. Keep in mind that leaders continued to go through this period without any metrics at all. The L&D manager produced a report showing the value of the program and gave it to his manager who said it passed his "weight test" because the report had multiple pages with charts and graphs and appendices. Because it weighed a lot, this manager never bothered to study it. The L&D manager was relieved that the report, although only cursorily read, was satisfactory. Upon leaving the office of his manager, his manager requested one thing: "Do this for all of our programs." The L&D manager froze. He could not do this for all programs. Yet the power for his manager was in seeing all the programs for the whole budget, not a fraction. The L&D manager had to explain that was not possible to do. They settled on roughly reasonable quantitative and qualitative data.

Figure 9: Required Level of Accuracy for Measurement

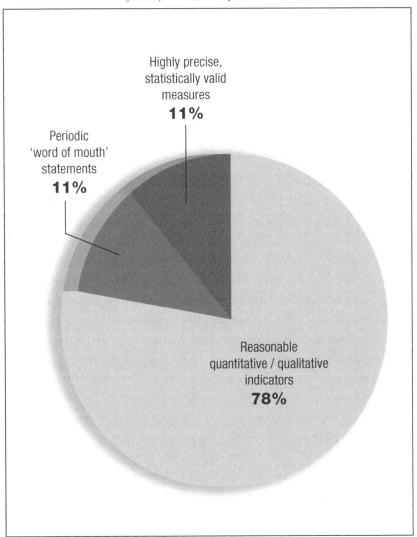

Highly precise,
statistically valid
measures
11%

Periodic
'word of mouth'
statements
11%

Reasonable
quantitative / qualitative
indicators
78%

Source: KnowledgeAdvisors, Learning Analytics Best Practices Research Study, 2004

Now that we understand what the research says, it really boils down to this: learning is the act of improving human capital performance, and those involved in learning must measure that improvement.

Learning impact, the key element that is desired by learning professionals, flows through three layers of impact:

1. Human capital
2. Business results
3. Stakeholder

Figure 10 shows a graphic representation of this impact flow. If learning is truly in the business of improving human capital, it is the most direct tie to impact and therefore the first bridge we must cross in measuring learning impact. Next, if human capital improves in its performance and productivity as a result of learning interventions, one indirect result will be an improvement in business results. At a macro level there are eight core business results indirectly impacted by learning investments:

1. Sales
2. Costs
3. Cycle time
4. Quality
5. Productivity
6. Employee retention
7. Customer satisfaction
8. Business risk

The ability to link learning to one or more of these results is important.

Finally, if business results improve, the business indicators will also move in the same direction — this is stakeholder value. For example, a public company that invests in L&D and in improving human capital should expect better business results and higher stock prices. There are even money management firms that invest only in companies that invest in people. Bassi Investments, led by Chair of the Board Laurie J. Bassi, PhD, does just this. Their investments consistently beat the S&P 500. Their example proves the learning impact flow.

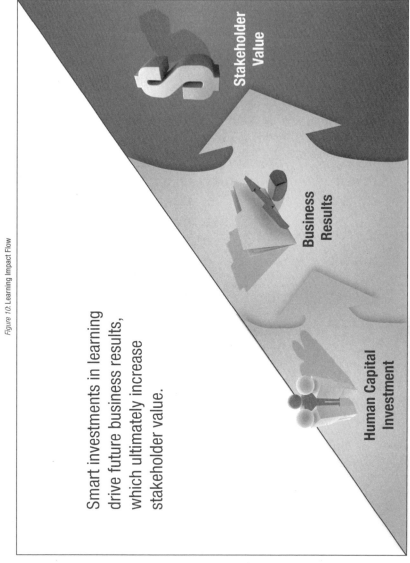

Figure 10: Learning Impact Flow

Smart investments in learning drive future business results, which ultimately increase stakeholder value.

Stakeholder Value

Business Results

Human Capital Investment

Source: KnowledgeAdvisors Learning Analytics Workshop Materials, 2005

Understanding that learning is in the business of improving human capital is a huge first step to measuring human capital. The next step is to understand all of the factors that affect the end result: increased stakeholder value.

The next five figures illustrate the transformation of the value of an organization and its human capital impact. If you measure human capital in this context, you will see how it fits into the bigger picture of the value of an organization.

Figure 11 shows that without learning, earnings will improve if you have appropriate processes and if you learn from mistakes. The improvement will be gradual, nearly straight-lined but with some upward slope.

Figure 12 compares the earnings of a firm with a solid learning program in which investment in human capital is made. Here we see an initial investment in learning that causes negative earnings initially, but over time the slope of the earnings growth is more dramatic than without the learning program. This illustrates the power of learning's impact on human capital, business results, and ultimately, earnings. Remember the Bassie fund.

Figure 13 presents an accounting indicator, the book value of a firm. Book value is assets less liabilities. The net assets represent the accounting value of the firm, also known as book value. Yet we know that companies like Coca-Cola, GE, and others are valued far higher than their accounting book value. This is seen in Figure 14. The market value, which, for public companies, is the stock price x shares outstanding, is higher than accounting book value or net assets. Why? Why would an investor pay more for a company than the sum of its net assets? The reason is the intangibles. Coca-Cola has a brand value. The name Coca-Cola is one of the most recognized on the planet. Investors would be willing to pay a premium over book value for that intangible.

Another intangible is an organization's human capital. The more productive the workforce the better the business results and, ultimately, the higher the market value. Figure 15 shows that some portion of the intangible is actually human capital value. This is the shaded area. This is the first item L&D professionals should try to measure. Why? Because L&D is in the business of improving human capital performance. Also, refer back to Figure 10. Isn't human capital investment the first and most direct link to L&D? This is why measuring human capital is important.

Figure 11. Earnings Without Learning

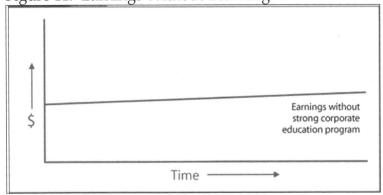

Source: KnowledgeAdvisors Learning Analytics
Workshop Materials, 2005

Figure 12. Earnings With Learning

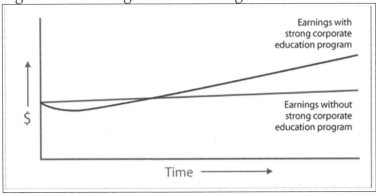

Source: KnowledgeAdvisors Learning Analytics
Workshop Materials, 2005

Figure 13. Book Value of an Organization

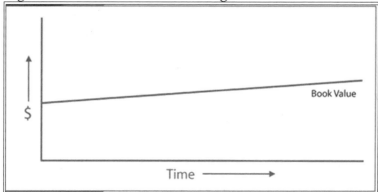

Source: KnowledgeAdvisors Learning Analytics
Workshop Materials, 2005

Figure 14. Book Value vs. Market Value

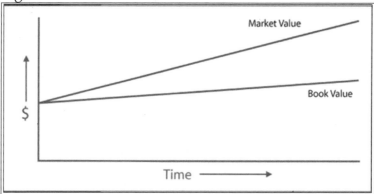

Source: KnowledgeAdvisors Learning Analytics
Workshop Materials, 2005

Figure 15. Human Capital Difference

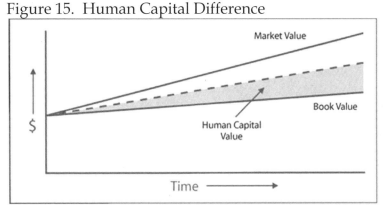

Source: KnowledgeAdvisors Learning Analytics
Workshop Materials, 2005

By now you are probably wondering if any of this
human capital measurement is really ever done or is
it just theory. Well, not so long ago Congress
questioned workforce development programs. They
wanted to know the ROI on future grants to develop
the workforce (i.e., human capital). This was not an
unreasonable question to ask. It is similar to how
executives question L&D organizations today.

Congress employed a well-known economist from the
University of Chicago, Dr. Gary Becker. Dr. Becker
studied the change in wage rates (a practical indicator
of the economic value of human capital) over time
tied to those segments where workforce development
funds (learning investments) had been injected. He
then used an economic formula to calculate the
impact of the programs on the wage rates and to
derive the human capital value. Dr. Becker was
essentially monetizing the shaded area in Figure 15.
His formula is illustrated in Figure 16.

Although the formula appears complex, it looks at the basics with some time elements attached. Wage rates are salary figures. "Marginal product" is the economist's term for change over time. The formula looks at the change due to the workforce development investments and factors in the cost of training. If you think this was not a credible or precise model, think again. Dr. Becker was awarded the Nobel Prize for his work on valuing human capital.

We propose that any L&D organization can do something similar. Leverage the right templates, ask the right questions. You don't need to be a Nobel-Prize-winning economist to learn from this and adapt it to your organization in a practical way.

Figure 16. Human Capital Valuation Formula

$$MP_0' + G \left[= \sum_{t=1}^{n-1} \frac{MP_t - W_t}{(1 + i)^t} \right] = W_0 + C$$

C = Cost of Training
MP = Marginal Product of Trainees
W = Wages Paid
G = Present Value of Returns
i = Market Discount Rate

Source: *Human Capital, A Theoretical and Empirical Analysis with Special Reference to Education*, 3rd Edition, Gary Becker

V. Human Capital Contribution Model™

If you're still hanging in there and ready to advance your thinking on human capital measurement, this chapter will go into detail on a model that will enable the learning organization to measure and improve business results and bottom-line impact.

Figure 17 illustrates the steps and flow of the model.

The Human Capital Contribution Model (HCCM) can achieve the following if applied:

- Ensure that business results are aligned with business objectives
- Significantly reduce wasted L&D expenses
- Substantially increase productivity
- Simplify the process of tracking actual business results
- Offer cost-effective approach to measuring ROI
- Enable you to link learning investments to bottom-line impact
- Provide data-driven approach to optimizing the impact of your L&D programs

So what is the business case for implementing a process and toolset like this? Without systems in place to track business impact, most organizations are not reaping the full benefits of their L&D investments. According to IDC, 50% of all training expenses are wasted. KnowledgeAdvisors research shows that

35% of people who go through learning programs do not apply what they learned, and perhaps more importantly, most learning programs could be improved to significantly increase productivity back on the job.

According to IDC, a typical Fortune 500 company or government agency invests approximately 2% of its revenue in L&D. If half is wasted, that means organizations on average waste 1% of revenue. Given this, if an organization has $5 billion in revenue than it is probably wasting $50 million per year. By implementing HCCM organizations can systematically drive out waste. In our example above, if waste is reduced by only 10% it will improve earnings by $500,000. The cost of implementing HCCM and its underlying technology, Metrics That Matter is approximately 1% of what an organization wastes in training.

By systematically finding ways to improve impact, organizations can significantly improve earnings. For example, if an organization with $1 billion in labor cost can increase productivity by just 1%, it will increase earnings by $10 million.

HCCM enables organizations to redirect wasted or poor-performing L&D investments into higher impact programs, which will significantly impact the bottom line.

Case Study Highlight: Defense Acquisition University (DAU) led by CLO of the Year Frank Anderson implemented a data-driven approach powered by Metrics That Matter, KnowledgeAdvisors' learning analytics technology, as its analytics engine.

Over the course of three years DAU was able to significantly increase output, effectiveness, and business impact without any increase in funding. This is a clear example of how an organization can systematically reduce waste and redirect investments into higher impact programs.

Figure 17: Human Capital Contribution Model™

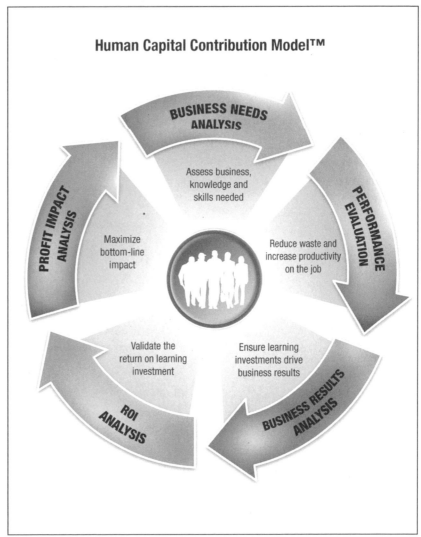

Source: KnowledgeAdvisors Human Capital Contribution Model™, 2005

Business Needs Analysis is the up-front planning process used to understand the business factors that are driving the creation of a learning and development program.

Why is this important? Because the key to a successful learning and development intervention that maximizes impact on the business begins with a formal analysis of business needs.

What's the process? To ensure that the right L&D investment is designed, developed, and delivered, a needs assessment should be conducted to understand the business objectives. Once identified, a knowledge and skill assessment should be conducted to examine the gap between the current state and the desired state.

What are the tools? The primary tools are needs assessments at the business and organizational levels, knowledge and skills assessments, pre- and post-tests, and competency assessments.

What are the results? Better designed learning programs and more clearly defined and measurable business objectives that can be linked to post-learning business results.

Performance Evaluation is a systematic approach to redirecting poor performing investments into programs that drive on-the-job productivity.

Why is this important? Because research has shown that nearly half (50%) of all training is wasted. In financial terms, for a typical Fortune 500 company that amounts to more than $50 million per year. More importantly, a typical Fortune 500 company could drive another $10 million in earnings if productivity were improved by 1%.

What's the process? To ensure that waste is eliminated and productivity continually improved, a systematic review of key indicators is needed to pinpoint the root cause of poor-performing investments. Performance analysis focuses on where the investment occurs (which programs? which courses? which vendors? which customers or lines of business?). It also analyzes key attributes of activity and performance data, including attendance rates, learning effectiveness, job impact, and value indicators.

What are the tools? Data sources for this analysis include LMS (learning management system) data and evaluation data. Using analytics tools like Metrics That Matter to collect, store, process, and report these results greatly facilitates the process.

What are the results? Better information for decision making. Future allocations of L&D resources to value-added programs, courses, vendors, and clients or lines of business will significantly impact the bottom line.

Business Result Analysis is a systematic approach to connecting L&D investments to a balanced set of actual results.

Why is this important? Because you can't manage what you don't measure. By systematically analyzing the link between learning and business results, one can identify areas for improvement and help drive better results. In addition, by analyzing business results, validation for ongoing investments can be made.

What's the process? HCCM is based on a balanced approach that is as closely aligned to financial statements as possible. After all, senior management performance is almost always based on financial results.

The recommended balanced set of business results most closely aligned with financial statements includes:

1. Revenue
2. Profitability
3. Productivity

This approach applies to both the public and private sector and is recommended for all major learning programs, including corporate universities, leadership programs, and business unit programs. When appropriate, it is also recommended that additional business results be tracked, such as quality, cycle time, employee loyalty, customer loyalty, and risk mitigation.

What are the tools? Data sources for this analysis include ERP (enterprise resource planning), financial and cost accounting, customer satisfaction, error rate, CRM (customer relationship management), and HRIS (human resource information systems). Tools like Metrics That Matter provide L&D managers with templates and wizards to analyze the key business results but are flexible enough to provide for customized business results analysis and to display the analysis on interpretive and graphical scorecards and dashboards.

What are the results? A thorough and timely understanding of organizational impact. L&D managers become advisors for improved performance.

ROI Analysis is a process-based approach to determining the financial return on L&D investments, given cost considerations.

Why is this important? Because investments should generate more positive financial value for the organization than the resources consumed in the original investment. It is also a commonly used financial analysis to validate investment decisions.

What's the process? To ensure that L&D management focuses on benefit vs. cost leveraging methodologies, such as Dr. Jack J. Phillips's ROI Process, to help provide a framework for ROI. The process of collecting, storing, processing, and reporting data that creates a monetary cost and benefit from training are inputs to the ROI Process, and isolating the benefit to training and adjusting it for bias and conservatism are part of the guiding principles of the ROI Process.

What are the tools? Data sources for this analysis include ERP (enterprise resource planning), financial and cost accounting, customer satisfaction, error rate, CRM (customer relationship management), and HRIS (human resource information systems). Tools like Metrics That Matter wrap automation, templates, and wizards around the Phillips ROI Process to make the administrative burden of ROI feasible and practical when there are limited resources.

What are the results? A credible and reliable ROI expressed as a benefit-to-cost ratio that, when compared with learning delivery, program, vendor, client, or line of business, will help the L&D manager make better decisions from a dual-dimensional perspective (benefit and cost). It will also validate the investment (or invalidate it in the case of a negative ROI).

Profit Impact Analysis is a data-driven planning and reporting process that helps to optimize the impact of L&D investments and to connect learning to financial statements.

Why is this important? Because L&D expense is part of the calculation, these profit measures are arguably the most meaningful ways to analyze past and future impact of learning on earnings.

What's the process? If learning intervention is effective, it will ultimately impact profit in a positive way. The financial goal of a corporate university is to increase the profit contribution of its people. Profit contribution can best be measured by taking revenue less labor costs and L&D expense, which is called the Human Capital Contribution Profit. A corporate university will be most successful when the Human Capital Contribution Profit is growing faster than the revenue, which is measured by calculating the Human Capital Contribution Margin (Human Capital Contribution Profit divided by Revenue).

What are the tools? Data sources for this analysis include financial and accounting systems. Tools like Metrics That Matter provide templates to guide a manager through the inputs and structured analysis to trend and track the actual to projected results.

What are the results? A sensitivity analysis tool that can help plan investments better and optimize L&D impact. It also enables learning professionals to discuss financial impact with business executives.

Business Needs Analysis

Core Diagnostic Tools

Like a doctor, an L&D consultant needs to ask the right questions before prescribing a solution. Just as the doctor uses basic medical devices such as thermometers and stethoscopes to gather initial data about the condition of a patient, an L&D consultant can use business needs assessments, tests, and competency tools to assess the health of a client in need.

The business needs assessment is a series of questions conducted via survey, interview, or focus group meant to identify the underlying reasons for an investment to be made in an improvement initiative. Business needs assessments are used before the learning intervention is designed. They are meant to understand the requirements and expectations as well as set appropriate L&D scope, given resources.

Figure 18 illustrates a needs assessment regarding customer satisfaction with a technology tool. Several users were asked to comment on their needs with respect to key elements of the technology and related service and support. From the assessment one can easily see the average results among the respondents for the major categories covered in the needs assessment. All areas are in need, but the greatest need is in technology functionality. If there are limited resources, this would be an area of higher priority, as that is where the greatest business need exists. To further refine the analysis, the analytics tool can drill down into each category to further pinpoint the specific area of greatest need.

Figure 18. Business Needs Assessment for Customer
Technology Needs: Example

Business Needs Assessment						
All Question	1	2	3	4	5	
My Average [n=822]						3.44
Communications	1	2	3	4	5	
My Average [n=597]						3.70
Customer Support	1	2	3	4	5	
My Average [n=633]						3.72
Overall Satisfaction	1	2	3	4	5	
My Average [n=789]						3.18
Satisfaction	1	2	3	4	5	
My Average [n=523]						3.32
Technology Functionality	1	2	3	4	5	
My Average [n=800]						3.21
Technology Performance	1	2	3	4	5	
My Average [n=797]						3.50
Training	1	2	3	4	5	
My Average [n=446]						3.80

Source: Metrics That Matter Learning Analytics
Technology by KnowledgeAdvisors

In addition to business needs assessments there are
knowledge and skill assessments. A common way of
measuring knowledge and skill is by a test. A pre-test
or a self-assessment can measure knowledge or skill
before the learning intervention and can be a useful
job aid to use before a learning intervention is ever
developed. Unlike a business needs assessment this
tool is designed to focus on human capital knowledge
or skill.

For example, in Figure 19 the L&D organization
created a simple test for the finance and accounting

organization to take prior to the creation of a learning program. The test was meant to determine whether the workforce had certain knowledge to accomplish the business need identified in the needs assessment. The test results revealed that only 38% of the finance and accounting employees had sufficient knowledge and skills as determined by test pass rates. In such a situation the L&D manager can conduct a more detailed item analysis on each test question to determine which questions were missed the most/least to further pinpoint the greatest skill gap.

Figure 19: Test Summary Report

Summary

Student	Test (100 points)	Test Score (100 points)	Test Pass (70 points)
jeff@ka.com	20	20	No
johnsmith@ka.com	40	40	No
maryjones@ka.com	20	20	No
philbrown@ka.com	60	60	No
sarasims@ka.com	100	100	Yes
bobcarson@ka.com	90	90	Yes
carolynjones@ka.com	70	70	Yes
jberk@cnatest.com	20	20	No
Average	**52.50**	**52.50**	**38%**

Test

Student	Combination Editi... (10 points)	A Journal Approve... (10 points)	In the new accoun... (10 points)	The preferred met... (10 points)	In the new accoun... (10 points)	People Soft simpli... (10 points)	Journals to be po... (10 points)
jeff@ka.com	0	0	0	0	0	10	10
johnsmith@ka.com	0	10	10	10	0	0	10
maryjones@ka.com	0	0	0	10	0	10	0
philbrown@ka.com	10	10	10	10	10	10	0
sarasims@ka.com	10	10	10	10	10	10	10
bobcarson@ka.com	10	10	0	10	10	10	10
carolynjones@ka.com	10	10	10	10	0	10	10

Source: Metrics That Matter Learning Analytics Technology by KnowledgeAdvisors

Finally, conducting competency assessments is a way to determine whether the workforce is strong enough in the required behaviors to carry out the business need. Competency assessments can be self-reported or done via manager, peer, or subordinate (i.e., 360 feedback). A competency tool in the area of leadership may have the following competencies that are the attributes of an effective leader: coaching, delegation, communication. The competency assessment measures areas where individuals or groups are strong, sufficient, or need improvement in certain behaviors that drive impact. Figure 20 shows the results of the leadership competency assessment. Communication is the area in which the most improvement needed.

Figure 20. Competency Assessment Output

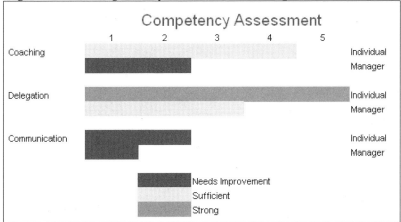

Source: KnowledgeAdvisors Competency Assessment Scorecard

Process for Business Needs Assessments

KnowledgeAdvisors suggests that every L&D organization create a set of organized steps to ensure a metric focus on identification of needs, knowledge, skills, and competencies.

At a high level, the following are the basic process steps for business needs analysis:

1. Prepare a business needs assessment at the organizational or individual level. Consider using standards. (KnowledgeAdvisors has standards to start from. If you'd like to use them, let us know!)
2. Collect, store, process, and report results.
3. Analyze results and identify areas of strongest business need, given resource constraints.
4. Prepare a knowledge- or skill-based test.
5. Collect, store, process, and report results.
6. Analyze results and identify areas of strongest skill gap.
7. Prepare a competency assessment for individuals and their managers.
8. Collect, store, process, and report results.
9. Analyze results and identify areas of strongest competency gap.
10. Based on strongest business need and largest skill and competency gaps, design, develop, and deliver targeted learning.

Performance Analysis

Waste Reduction

KnowledgeAdvisors research shows that *81% of all L&D measurement resources are administrative in nature.* This means the vast majority of resources are allocated toward readying data for analysis versus decision making. Analytics tools are designed to collect, store, process, and report data. This frees the analyst for information decision making. See Figure 19 for an illustration of the activities taking place when readying the data for analysis where Metrics That Matter reduced administrative burden.

A great first step in managing investments in human capital performance is to identify opportunities for waste reduction. This primarily falls into three categories:

1. Reduction of administrative costs to properly evaluate programs
2. Reduction of infrequently used resources
3. Replacement of suboptimal training solutions

Reducing administrative costs is an easy first step. Integrations between analytics technologies and feeder systems such as learning management systems (LMS) allow automation and interoperability between systems. This saves duplicate data entry and paper processing, and automates storage, processing, and reporting. See Figure 21 for a schematic of a typical integration between a learning analytics tool, Metrics That Matter, and a learning management system.

Figure 21: Integration of LMS with Analytics Technologies

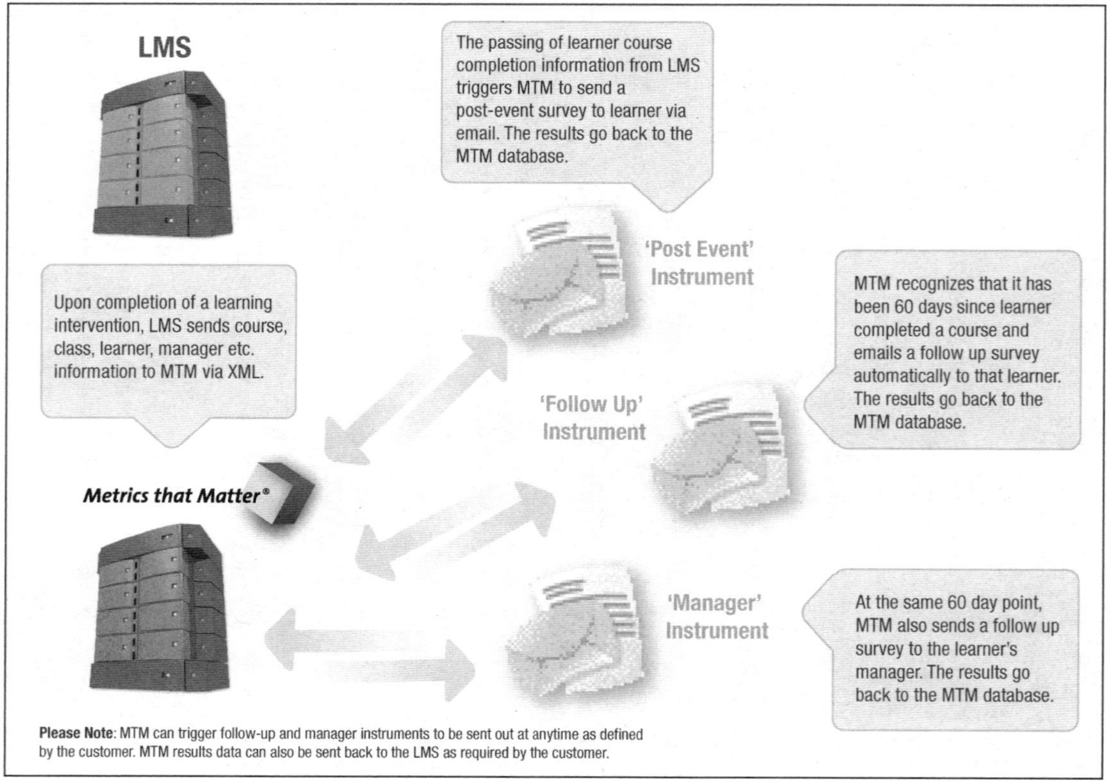

LMS

Upon completion of a learning intervention, LMS sends course, class, learner, manager etc. information to MTM via XML.

The passing of learner course completion information from LMS triggers MTM to send a post-event survey to learner via email. The results go back to the MTM database.

'Post Event' Instrument

MTM recognizes that it has been 60 days since learner completed a course and emails a follow up survey automatically to that learner. The results go back to the MTM database.

'Follow Up' Instrument

'Manager' Instrument

At the same 60 day point, MTM also sends a follow up survey to the learner's manager. The results go back to the MTM database.

Metrics that Matter®

Please Note: MTM can trigger follow-up and manager instruments to be sent out at anytime as defined by the customer. MTM results data can also be sent back to the LMS as required by the customer.

Source: KnowledgeAdvisors Integration Process

Beyond systems integrations, a key to waste reduction is to identify the elements of measurement that are administrative versus value-added and then to leverage technology and templates to reduce administration. Resources can then be saved for data analysis. Figure 22 shows the administrative elements of learning analytics. Within each step, pinpoint technology leverage and templates. For example, in data collection use Internet technologies versus paper to collect an evaluation.

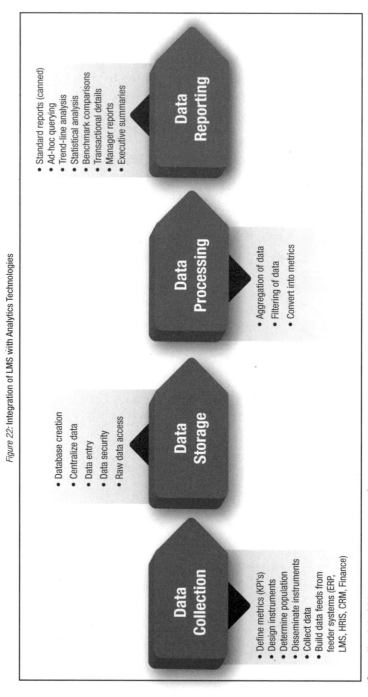

Figure 22: Integration of LMS with Analytics Technologies

Data Collection
- Define metrics (KPI's)
- Design instruments
- Determine population
- Disseminate instruments
- Collect data
- Build data feeds from feeder systems (ERP, LMS, HRIS, CRM, Finance)

Data Storage
- Database creation
- Centralize data
- Data entry
- Data security
- Raw data access

Data Processing
- Aggregation of data
- Filtering of data
- Convert into metrics

Data Reporting
- Standard reports (canned)
- Ad-hoc querying
- Trend-line analysis
- Statistical analysis
- Benchmark comparisons
- Transactional details
- Manager reports
- Executive summaries

Source: KnowledgeAdvisors

Reducing under-utilized resources is another waste reduction mechanism. KnowledgeAdvisors research studies show that nearly 75% of organizations investing in an e-Learning library utilize less than 30% of the library. By default, most organizations under-utilize e-Learning libraries.

The key to reducing waste with under-utilized resources is to identify the resources and analyze the root cause of under-utilization. Resources to consider in an L&D operation include:

- Instructor workforce
- Physical training locations
- Courseware completions

For example, change suboptimal training solutions where waste reduction can occur. It is vital to trend and track indicators of poorer performance. Reviewing some of the following can help with waste reduction and reallocation of resources:

- Areas where there is little actual application of training on the job
- Courses or business units with high percentages of low learning effectiveness (indicates the right people were not in the training or that training is weak)
- Areas with low alignment between training content and business outcomes
- Identification of barriers to impact of training on the job

In Figure 23, a table from Metrics That Matter illustrates application on the job and barriers to utilization for a corporate university over a month of organization-wide training. This data was collected sixty days later, automatically by the technology, to understand when application happened (if at all) and if not, why not. There is 14% waste (where training had not yet applied) and the biggest barrier was lack of opportunity. Trending this data over time or by key programs can help in waste reduction.

Figure 23: Job Impact and Barriers to Impact

	Follow Up
Respondents in Data Analysis	**1068**

Time to Job Impact	Follow Up
1 Week	42.11%
2-4 Weeks	32.98%
5-6 Weeks	10.84%
I haven't applied what I learned yet, but I plan to	12.07%
I don't expect to use the knowledge/skills gained	2.00%

Barriers to Use	Follow Up
Content not practical	12.02%
Prevented or discouraged from using	3.83%
No opportunity	56.64%
Other high priorities	20.77%
Did not deploy technology or program	N/A
Other	20.77%

Source: Metrics That Matter Learning Analytics Technology by KnowledgeAdvisors

Another example of waste reduction is an analytic output such as Facility Utilization Ratio (Figure 24). A manager looking at waste reduction can see that the Chicago site is the one most utilized and that several locations have only one training day. This information can lead to decisions to consolidate or close physical training locations that are under-utilized. However, if this data is hard to obtain or not tracked, these low-hanging opportunities will be missed.

Figure 24: Facility Utilization

Facility Utilization in Number of Training Days

Run By: Customer Satisfaction (customer) . . . . MTM Tool: Training Utilization

Date Run: October 27, 2005 . . . . From Saved Query: No.

	No. of Training Days
Bangkok	2
Boston, MA	1
Chicago, IL	5
Client Site	2
Hyatt Regency San Francisco Airport	1
KA - Chicago, IL	2
Kuala Lumpur	2
Madison, WI	2
Reston, VA.	1
Waverly, IA	1

Source: Metrics That Matter Learning Analytics Technology by KnowledgeAdvisors

Performance Improvement

Investment analysis should also cover performance improvement. An optimized investment not only reduces waste but also continuously improves its process, making it more efficient and effective.

Performance improvement is complementary to changing a suboptimal training solution. An L&D manager should look at the following types of indicators for ensuring that the L&D process is continuing to deliver value-added training and improves upon doing so:

- Review quality indicators, which include (a) instructor performance, (b) courseware quality, and (c) environment conduciveness to learning
- Review knowledge transfer indicators, which include (a) pre- and post-test results and (b) evaluation indicators of training from the students' perception
- Review behavior change on the job that could be gained from observation, follow-up evaluation, and managerial evaluation
- Review alignment with business results: if sales training occurred, did sales increase?

Using analytics technologies like Metrics That Matter to slice the aforementioned data by course, program, vendor, instructor, business unit, job function, office location, years of service, etc. can provide for profiles of learners and training to pinpoint performance improvement opportunities.

In Figure 25, the data shows the effectiveness of impact courseware. The easy-to-read analysis shows the red items that should alert an L&D manager to take action. In this case, if we find that incorrect prerequisites exist or that the content lacks real-world, relevant examples and is not current, we will likely find the culprit behind poor performance. But the data highlighted where to look. In business when resources are limited, rely on the right data to guide you.

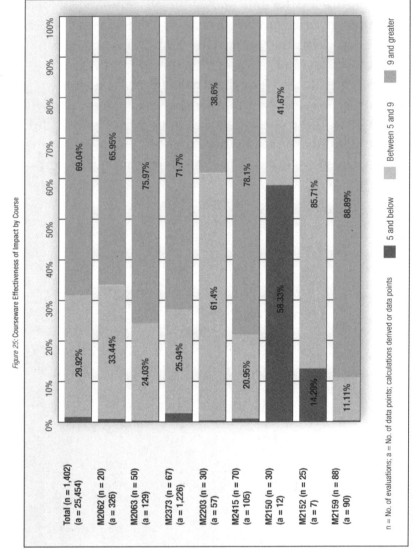

Figure 25: Courseware Effectiveness of Impact by Course

n = No. of evaluations; a = No. of data points; calculations derived or data points

Source: Metrics That Matter Learning Analytics Technology by KnowledgeAdvisors

Another example is the analysis of impact by line of business. Performance improvement analysis needs attributes of the participant, not just the training, to be identifiable and actionable. In Figure 26 we see data for the impact that training had on the job several months later, sorted by job function at a typical organization. The R&D group has had little job impact compared to the HR and IT groups. This type of data can help the L&D management understand which areas of their business have significant performance improvement opportunities.

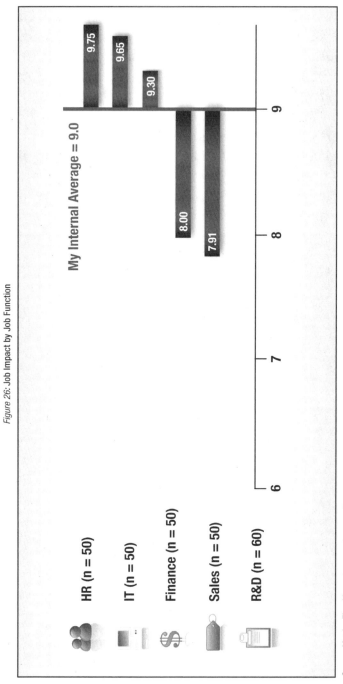

Figure 26: Job Impact by Job Function

Source: Metrics That Matter Learning Analytics Technology by KnowledgeAdvisors

Process for Waste Reduction and Performance Improvement

KnowledgeAdvisors suggests that every L&D organization create a set of organized steps to ensure a metric focus on waste reduction and performance improvement.

At a high level, the following are some basic process steps for performance analysis:

1. Identify the most strategic, costly, and visible programs.
2. Identify the elements of the L&D organization that will be enablers of these programs. These elements include the financial, physical, and human resources allocated to these programs.
3. Construct a list of key performance indicators for the activity (how many were trained) and performance (how well we trained) attributes of these programs.
    a. Activity KPI examples
        i. Location utilization
        ii. Instructor training days
        iii. Courseware utilization by delivery
        iv. Number of completions to enrollments
    b. Performance KPI examples
        i. Instructor performance
        ii. Courseware quality
        iii. Location conduciveness to learning

      iv. Learning effectiveness /
           Knowledge transfer
      v. Weeks to apply training
      vi. Barriers to application
      vii. Alignment with business results
      viii. Perceived training value

4. Determine practical data sources and collection mechanisms.
5. Identify a central database for storage of the data.
6. Automate the processing of the raw data into KPIs by program.
7. Review the KPIs on a regular basis against (a) trends of prior periods, (b) realistic yet challenging goals, and (c) internal and external benchmarks.
8. Based on analysis, drill down into data to find the root cause of waste or poor performance. Drill down by:
   c. Class
   d. Course
   e. Curricula
   f. Instructor
   g. Vendor
   h. Learning delivery
   i. Location of delivery
   j. Attribute of the participant (years of service, job role, business unit, geographic location)
9. Prioritize improvement opportunities based on resources available for improvements. Focus first on items requiring little resources and change management (e.g., change prerequisites

for a leadership course from 5 years to 10
years). Next focus on areas where automation
and technology could play a role (e.g.,
implement an automated and integrated
technology to cut down on L&D
administration). Finally, focus on long-term
solutions like a complete revamp of a major
program.
10. Continue to monitor and measure the KPIs to
ensure that changes remain in effect.

Business Results Analysis

The Challenges with Business Results Analysis

The first step in business results analysis is to
understand which results are important to
management and which drive the business and create
shareholder value. Profitability analysis focuses more
directly on shareholder value. Secondly, tracking
these results for a key program is necessary to ensure
that a strategic, visible, or costly program was in fact
aligned with the business results driving the need for
the program. Thirdly, tracking macro results on a
continual basis and being able to link the results to
training can help an L&D manager understand where
a learning intervention positively, negatively, or
neutrally affected the end result. This not only helps
an L&D manager to decide future resource allocation
but also to educate the stakeholder about the
predicted or actual effect of training (this is known as

isolation and will be discussed further in ROI analysis).

Business results analysis faces several challenges. It is essential that the L&D manager clearly recognize the challenges before engaging in business results analysis. Common challenges to business results analysis include the following:

- L&D does not have the appropriate competencies to consult with the stakeholder, identify the results, and analyze the L&D effect on them.
- L&D does not have the money or time to allocate to a comprehensive analysis of business results tied to every key program.
- There is no direct and clear link to a specific business result for the L&D intervention. For example, a leadership program may be established to increase delegation skills and coaching skills, but it is not intended to promote sales growth directly.
- The stakeholder does not have or is not willing to provide the resources to work with L&D to perform a business results analysis (yet the stakeholder wants to know the business results link anyway).
- The actual business results data does not exist or does not exist in a format that can be used for analysis purposes (i.e., garbage in would be garbage out).
- There is no formal system or database that houses the business results that would then automatically pull into an analytics system on a regular basis for analysis.

Do these challenges imply that the L&D manager has an acceptable excuse not to analyze business results but to simply ignore them? HCCM strongly argues against this practice.

KnowledgeAdvisors Recommended Actual Business Results

To overcome the aforementioned challenges of measuring business results, HCCM will present a practical, scalable, and repeatable way of measuring business results. HCCM has a recommended set of core business results *any* L&D department should consider tracking, regardless of the specific programs or micro business results that may be currently tracked. KnowledgeAdvisors utilized its experience in financial analysis with banking and accounting personnel who understand how to read and interpret financial statements to derive the recommended actual business results. Based on this collective wisdom, KnowledgeAdvisors believes that by building data feeds or simply inputting five data points on a quarterly basis, a robust scorecard can be generated that illustrates real income statement impacts in terms of **growth, productivity, and profitability**, derived from L&D investments. These business results—growth, productivity and profitability—are the *metrics that matter* to senior managers.

The inputs necessary for growth, productivity, and profitability business results require only five simple inputs, which are as follows:

1. Revenue — directly from income statement financial data or from sales/financial systems
2. Number of employees — directly from notes to financial statement data or from HRIS systems
3. Labor cost / total payroll expense — directly from income statement financial data or notes to financial statements or from payroll systems
4. Number of learners — directly from LMS information or registration data
5. Actual L&D expense — L&D organizations should be able to give this figure to accounting departments when closing general ledgers

As a result of inputting or establishing a regular data feed for these inputs between the feeder system and the analytics technology, an L&D manager can derive:

Growth: [{Current period revenue – Prior period revenue} / Prior period revenue].

Growth is a key indicator that shows revenue change against goal or period to period. This allows an L&D manager to understand fluctuation in revenue and to immediately recognize a critical point.

Productivity: [Current period revenue / # of employees]

This particular productivity indicator is revenue per employee. Best-practice organizations should be able to increase revenue with steady or fewer employees due to better process, technologies, and training.

Analysis of productivity can be a significant factor in understanding both the revenue and the cost side of the profit impact equation. Revenue is inherent in its numerator and number of employees in the denominator. The monetary value of personnel is an expense on the income statement. Business decisions should be made with revenue per employee in mind. If the number is declining, it means revenue is not keeping pace with employee additions. If the number is improving, it indicates the processes, technologies, and people are generating more revenue without increasing human capital at the same rate.

Profitability: [Sales – {Payroll expense + L&D expense} / Sales]

KnowledgeAdvisors refers to the profitability metric as the Human Capital Contribution Margin. Financial analysis relies on margin analysis to tell us what is left over from sales after expenses are covered. To an L&D manager the expenses are human capital. Two major human capital expenses exist: (a) payroll expense and (b) L&D expense.

This calculation should be monitored closely by L&D managers. It helps them understand how much revenue is left over after human capital expenses (which directly hit the income statement) are covered. Organizations with high human capital contribution margins are indicative of productive organizations that generate the most revenue without increasing human capital expenses at the same rate as revenue. On the contrary, lower margins indicate opportunities for improvement. They tell us that sales growth is not aligned with human capital growth. They indicate that human capital performance is not optimized.

A visual dashboard can be generated that illustrates these vital business results as well as some complementary metrics that should be reviewed in conjunction with growth, productivity, and profitability. See Figure 27 for a visual of this dashboard, which can measure actual results period to period or against goals. The dashboard can be generated from an analyst inputting the data into templates or setting up a system link to feeder systems that automatically populate the input templates.

To round out the dashboard, in addition to growth, productivity, and profitability, we review L&D actual expenses and L&D activity. If the number of learners completing training is increasing while L&D budget is held constant or decreasing and while human capital contribution margin is increasing, that suggests a highly effective L&D organization optimizing its resources. So these additional two metrics are part of the standard KnowledgeAdvisors Actual Business Results Dashboard.

By tracking these actual and recommended business results and computing KPIs tied to real financial statement results, an L&D manager can directly see how his or her budget and the actions taken with the budget can influence the income statement and profitability of the organization.

Figure 27. Actual Business Results Dashboard with Default Profit Impact Metrics

92

Figure 27: Actual Business Results Dashboard - Visual Summary of Actual Business Results

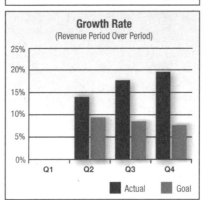

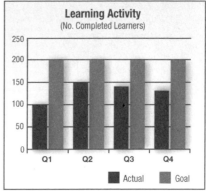

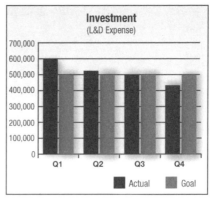

Source: KnowledgeAdvisors Actual Business Results Dashboard

Analyzing and Improving Business Results Program by Program

Notwithstanding the KnowledgeAdvisors actual business results that link to the income statement and profitability, there are potentially hundreds if not thousands of micro business results an L&D manager could track or for which an L&D manager could be held accountable. For example, a macro result such as quality has micro results such as reduced transaction errors, lower safety incidents, or improved evaluation scores for courseware ratings.

Beginning with a macro set of business results and tracking those against key programs is a valuable way to understand where L&D is aligned with results. KnowledgeAdvisors research identifies eight core business reasons why organizations invest in learning:

1. Increased revenues
2. Decreased costs
3. Increased productivity
4. Increased quality
5. Decreased cycle time
6. Increased customer satisfaction
7. Increased employee retention
8. Decreased risk

Any manager with a significant budget should be held accountable for the budgets link to results that drive the business. Accountability is a key driver in resource allocations in business today. It is so critical that the U. S. federal government changed the name of the General Accounting Office (GAO) to the Government Accountability Office (GAO).

So the question is, how does L&D obtain business results when challenges (like those mentioned previously) exist? The answer is, there are many ways to do this. We will explore them now:

1. Modify evaluations to include a linkage to business results. This takes advantage of where natural data collection in the existing process occurs. Figure 28 shows how the macro results mentioned above are evaluated across all programs to be viewed on a scorecard. In this example, over 12,000 respondents are rating the alignment of the L&D program to macro results. Sales had the lowest alignment at 28%. This L&D manager was able to make adjustments to programs to increase this percentage over time, as sales increases were core profitability metrics.

Figure 28: Business Results Alignment

Respondents in Data Analysis	12132
Results	
Expect the program will significantly impact increasing quality	66.96%
Expect the program will significantly impact decreasing costs	71.77%
Expect the program will significantly impact decreasing cycle time	63.42%
Expect the program will significantly impact increasing productivity	80.80%
Expect the program will significantly impact increasing sales	28.84%
Expect the program will significantly impact increasing customer satisfaction	60.25%
Expect the program will significantly impact increasing employee satisfaction	58.95%

Source: Metrics That Matter Learning Analytics Technology by KnowledgeAdvisors

Use technology to create conditional questions that show the significance in terms of business results. Figure 29 shows how a technology company was able to understand in more detail how business results linked to technology training improved on-the-job performance. In the following example, productivity, quality, and customer satisfaction are most impacted by the training. The Metrics That Matter technology factors into the result the training effect and the adjustment for bias in analysis (more of this is covered in the ROI Analysis section).

2.

Figure 29: Training Impact on Business Results

Business Results: Productivity (analyze and monetize this result)	Post Event
Total percent improvement in productivity, including training	51%
Training's contribution to improved productivity	57%
Percent improvement due to training	29.1%
Adjustment factor for confidence in estimations	65%
Adjusted percent improvement due to training	18.9%

Business Results: Quality (analyze and monetize this result)	Post Event
Total percent improvement in quality, including training	54%
Training's contribution to improved quality	57%
Percent improvement due to training	30.8%
Adjustment factor for confidence in estimations	65%
Adjusted percent improvement due to training	20%

Business Results: Increasing Customer Satisfaction (analyze and monetize this result)	Post Event
Total percent improvement in customer satisfaction, including training	52%
Training's contribution to improved customer satisfaction	57%
Percent improvement due to training	29.6%
Adjustment factor for confidence in estimations	65%
Adjusted percent improvement due to training	19.3%

Source: Metrics That Matter Learning Analytics Technology by KnowledgeAdvisors

Compare actual business results against goals and trends. L&D managers should be aware of key drivers. Trends are important. In addition to the analysis, color-coding it to facilitate interpretation and action is just as important as the data collection itself. In Figure 30 the L&D manager is able to track actual results important to the organization. It trends the inputs period-over-period and against goals. The color-coding shows where variances exceed 10% in a positive or negative direction (red = negative, green = positive, and yellow = neutral.) If the result is to be analyzed on a regular basis, the inputs can be imported into the learning analytics technology via pre-arranged data feeds.

Figure 30: Actual Business Results Scorecard with Trends, Goals, and Color Analysis

Actual Business Results		Q1	Q2	Q3	Q4
Quality (Error Rates in PPM)	*Actual*	—	-8.33%	18.18%	-92.31%
Days to Close a Sale	*Actual*	—	-6.67%	-28.57%	24.00%
Goals		Q1	Q2	Q3	Q4
Quality (Error Rates in PPM)	*Goal*	—	-9.09%	-40.00%	-33.33%
Days to Close a Sale	*Goal*	—	-2.78%	-7.14%	-7.69%

3.

Source: KnowledgeAdvisors Actual Business Results Scorecard

4. Track the business results specific to each strategic, visible, or costly program. This ensures that in addition to tracking results at a macro/organizational level, L&D is able to drill into key results for key programs. Figure 31 illustrates how an L&D manager can link a sales program to sales revenues by tracking sales before and after training. To make the analysis more credible additional analysis is also tracked. Additional analysis includes control group comparison and a root-cause (isolation) analysis as well as a bias factor adjustment. A tool like Figure 31 is an excellent consultative tool for L&D to use when partnering with lines of business to understand L&D effects on business results.

5. Dashboards are great visual aids. Ensuring that the key business results are not only placed on scorecards but also on summary dashboards is important for executives in L&D to ensure that the metrics are top of mind. Figure 32 displays a few of the dashboard items that aid in KnowledgeAdvisors Actual Business Results analysis, which was strongly recommended as the core results to track. Dashboards are effective if they represent a small subset of metrics that are relevant and easy to interpret, and display trend and goal comparisons.

Figure 31: Technology Template for Inputs of Actual Business Results by Strategic Program

1) Name your worksheet: `Sales Training`

2) Name the business result (ex. increased quality, annualized) `Increased Sales, annualized`

3) Define your business result performance measure (ex. Defects per unit, annualized) `Sales Revenue per year`

4) Estimate the quantitative metric for each performance measure:

Important note: all items in this section must be annualized (ex. 1 month of data is 100 unit sales representing $1000, input 1200 unit sales representing $12,000 as an annualized number).

	Group Trained Metric	Monetary Value	Control Group Metric (Optional)	Monetary Value
Estimate the metric as measured **BEFORE** the training:	100	10000	100	10000
Estimate the metric as measured **AFTER** the training:	150	15000	110	11000
Total change in metric:	50%	5000	10%	1000

5) Isolate root causes of the total percentage change in metric.

Please input the percentage of the change in the metric that was driven by these causes (total should equal 100%)

	Group Trained Metric	Monetary Value	Control Group Metric (Optional)	Monetary Value
Personnel:	0	0	0	0
Technology:	20	1000	20	200
External factors:	0	0	0	0
Procedure / Policy:	30	1500	50	500
Incentives:	0	0	0	0
Training:	50	2500	0	0
Other:	0	0	30	300
Total (should equal 100%)	100%	5000	100%	1000

6) Adjustment factor for confidence in estimations: (percentage) `65`

	Percent	Monetary Value
7) Percent change isolated to Training: (Adjusted for confidence)	16%	1625

Source: Metrics That Matter Learning Analytics Technology by KnowledgeAdvisors

Figure 32: Business Results Displayed in Dashboard Format

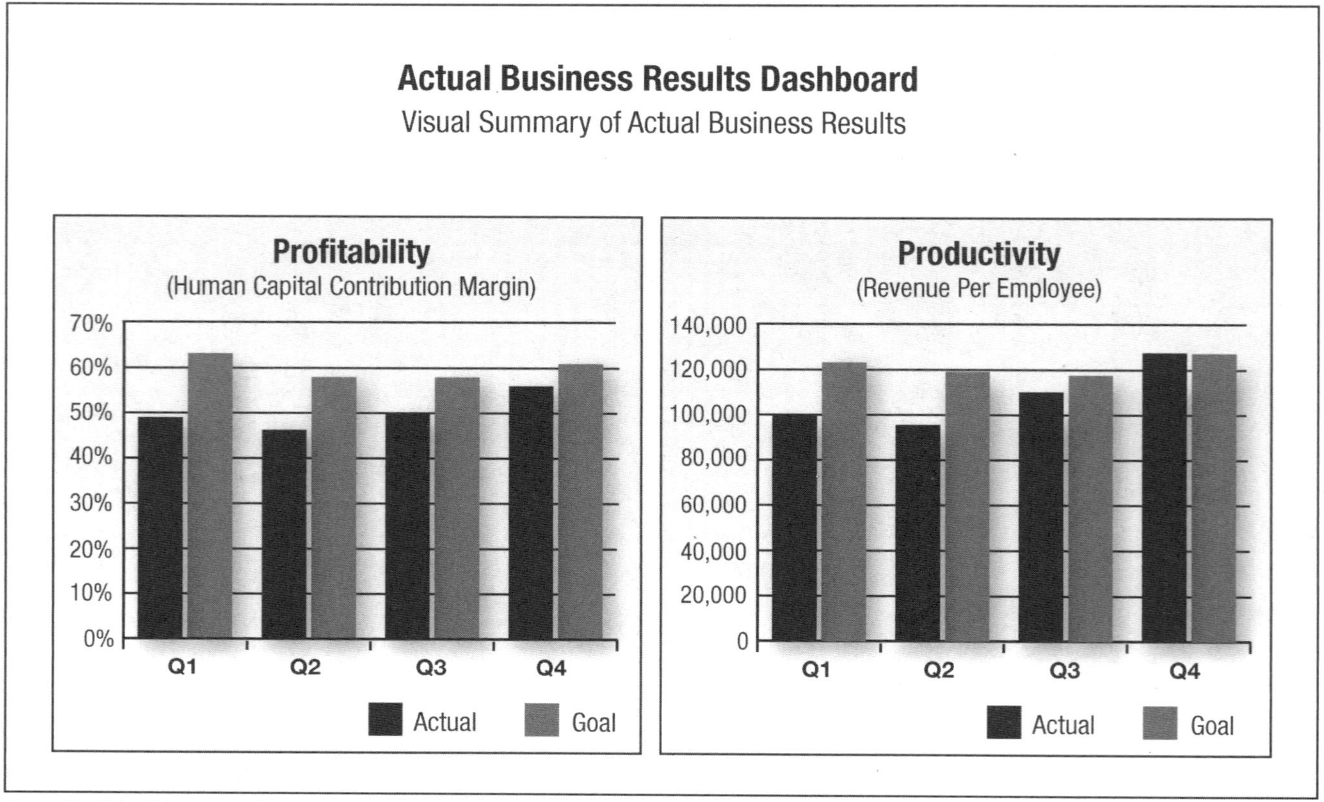

Actual Business Results Dashboard
Visual Summary of Actual Business Results

Profitability
(Human Capital Contribution Margin)

Productivity
(Revenue Per Employee)

Source: KnowledgeAdvisors Actual Business Results Scorecard

Process for Business Results Analysis

KnowledgeAdvisors suggests that every L&D organization create a set of organized steps to ensure a metric focus to track and trend business results

At a high level, the following are some basic process steps for Business Results Analysis:

1. Identify the business results that are financial statement drivers (most significant results). KnowledgeAdvisors suggests the following:
   a. Growth
   b. Productivity per employee (as measured by revenue per employee)
   c. Profitability (as measured by human capital contribution margin, which is revenue less labor cost plus L&D expense)
2. Identify macro business results that drive investments in L&D or any other resource allocation. KnowledgeAdvisors suggests the following:

   d. Increased revenues
   e. Decreased costs
   f. Increased productivity
   g. Increased quality
   h. Decreased cycle time
   i. Increased customer satisfaction
   j. Increased employee retention
   k. Decreased risk

3. Identify the most strategic, costly, and visible programs and identify the business results that should be outcomes of those programs.
4. Once all financial, macro, and program-specific results are identified, determine, with regard to available financial, physical, and human resources, how the data will be collected.

    l. Collect data on evaluation forms
    m. Collect data using action-plan templates (see ROI Analysis for further details)
    n. Collect data via templatized, consultative input forms
    o. Collect data via automated data imports from feeder systems (sales, finance, etc.)

5. Identify a central database for storage of the data.
6. Automate the processing of the raw data into KPIs by program.
7. Review the KPIs on a regular basis against (a) trends of prior periods, (b) realistic yet challenging goals, and (c) internal and external benchmarks.
8. Based on analysis, drill down into data to find the root cause of trend and goal variances. Drill down by:

    p. Class
    q. Course
    r. Curricula
    s. Instructor
    t. Vendor
    u. Learning delivery
    v. Location of delivery

  w. Attribute of the participant (years of
    service, job role, business unit,
    geographic location)
9. Prioritize where L&D investments should be
 increased, decreased, or maintained at existing
 levels, based on root cause and variance
 analysis.
10. Continue to monitor and measure the KPIs to
  ensure alignment of resource allocations with
  changes in business results.

ROI Analysis

The Phillips ROI Process Model

In most departments there is a need to justify or
validate the training cost. In L&D it is no different. If
an organization has limited resources, ROI Analysis
can help the organization validate the investment.

In the mid 1980s Dr. Jack J. Phillips developed the
Phillips ROI Process. It has since helped hundreds of
organizations to prepare ROI analysis on strategic,
visible, and costly L&D programs. Figure 33 shows
the flow of the Phillips ROI Process. It begins with
organizing what, how, and when data will be
collected, followed by an isolation of results to
training, a conversion to monetary value, and the ROI
calculation itself.

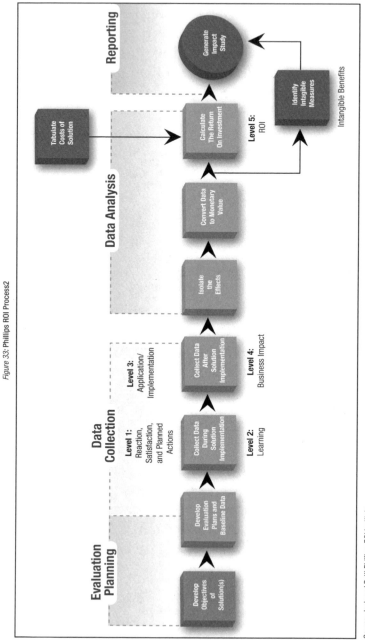

Figure 33: Phillips ROI Process2

Source: Jack and Patti Phillips, ROI Institute

Phillips has a set of best practices referred to as "Guiding Principles." A key guiding principle to the ROI Process is Estimation, Isolation, and Adjustment. This has added tremendous value to ROI Analysis for L&D managers.

For example, consider a sales training program and the use of Estimation/Isolation/Adjustment to derive an ROI (in the form of a benefit-to-cost ratio) for the program:

- Training cost for program: $15,000
- Improvement measure significantly impacted: sales
- Define measure and its unit of measure: 1 closed sale
- **Estimate** value of 1 unit of improvement in the measure. For example, the value of a closed sale is sales value times the profit margin ($10,000 x 20% = $2,000)
- State basis for value of 1 unit of improvement. For example, standard cost or sales price
- How much the unit will improve in performance and frequency: 4 sales per month
- **Isolate** performance improvement due to training: 60%
- **Adjust** for bias, confidence, conservatism: 65%
- Calculate monetized benefit: $2000 x4 x12 = $96,000 in total sales improvement annualized
- Adjust for isolation to training and confidence: 96,000 x60% x65% = 27,690
- Calculate ROI: $27,690 - $15,000 = $12,690

- Calculate Benefit-to-Cost Ratio: $27,690/15,000 = 1.85

By investigating each element of this principle we can see that Estimation is merely stating the change in the business result. In the Business Results Analysis section we discussed the need to constantly track core results and to track results on a program-by-program level. The Business Results Analysis is a feeder into the ROI Analysis.

Isolation is a next step. There are many variables that drive the change in a business result. If an L&D organization desires to show a specific ROI on a business result, it must factor out the variables that impacted the result but were not L&D-related. KnowledgeAdvisors has tools to help in the isolation exercise and has identified major root cause factors for isolation, which include the following:

1. People
2. Process
3. Technology
4. Culture
5. Externalities
6. Measurements
7. L&D program

The training variable should be the main focus in an L&D ROI Analysis. The other factors may drive the business result as well, but L&D managers are interested in their part of the result variance.

Dr. Phillips also discusses various isolation techniques. The more rigorous techniques are preferable but less frequently used, because they are more costly and time- consuming. Isolation techniques include the following:

1. Control group analysis
2. Trend line analysis
3. Statistical analysis
4. Participant, manager, or expert estimation

The fourth isolation technique is most frequently used although it is not as credible as the others. Thus, the ROI Process takes into account a final factor: adjustment. Adjustment accounts for imperfections in the analysis, self-reported bias, lack of confidence, and conservatism. It is a factor by which the impact from L&D on a business result is reduced.

KnowledgeAdvisors deploys the principles of Estimation/Isolation/Adjustment into its ROI models. Their learning analytics technology, Metrics That Matter, is the only tool in the marketplace endorsed by Dr. Jack Phillips because of its integration of the ROI Process into the design of ROI tools and calculations.

Figure 34 shows a KnowledgeAdvisors ROI calculation from its proprietary Human Capital ROI Card. The technology derived the monetary benefit in Figure 34 by automatically performing an Estimation / Isolation / Adjustment calculation on the input data — in this example, evaluation data received at the end of a program. The user of the technology then input the cost of the program and the average salary levels of program participants (the monetary value of human capital) to derive the ROI. Technology wrapped around credible process and methodology makes the ROI Analysis easier to do. Once the ROI is generated, comparing it by program, vendor, client, line of business, and learning delivery helps in deciding resource allocation.

Figure 34: Human Capital ROI Score Card

Human Capital ROI Score Card

Level 5 Return on Investment	Post Event
Costs (per person)	1,000
Monetary Benefits (per person)	3,500
Benefit to Cost Ratio	3.5
ROI Percentage	250%
Payback Period (months)	3.43

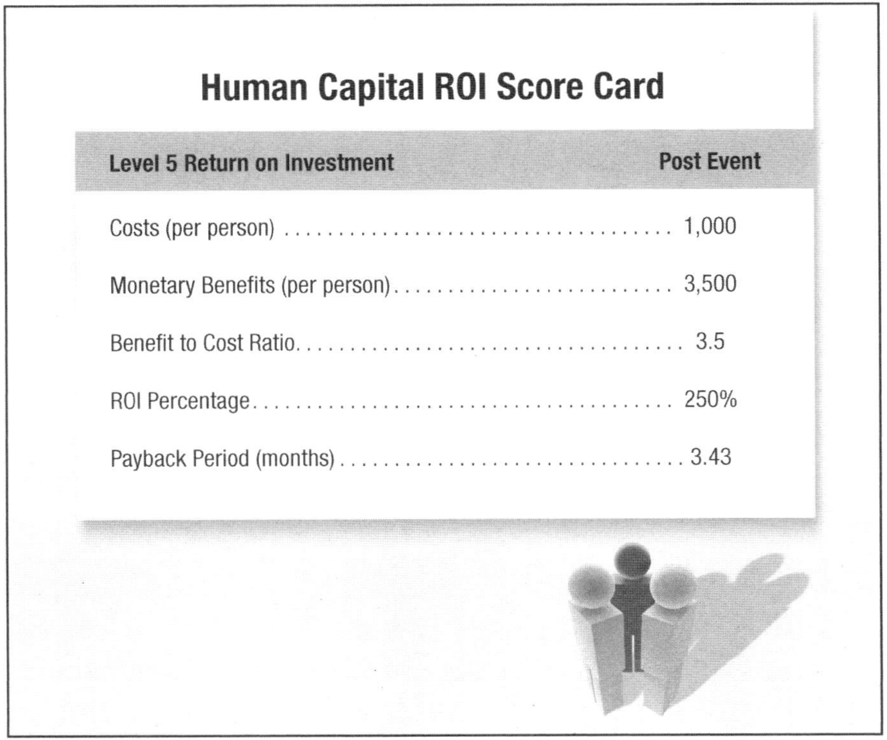

Source: Metrics That Matter Learning Analytics Technology by KnowledgeAdvisors

Dr. Jack Phillips has worked closely with KnowledgeAdvisors to incorporate specific tools and templates into the Metrics That Matter Learning Analytics Technology. The primary elements that can save significant time in conducting ROI Analysis are in the automated tabulation of costs, benefits, and summary scorecards while maintaining the integrity of the ROI Process.

Figure 35 illustrates a key feature of ROI Analysis, the tabulation of costs. Costs are typically comprised of the following cost components:
- Tuition
- Analysis
- Development
- Acquisition
- Delivery
- Evaluation
- Overhead
- Participant opportunity

Conservatism in cost analysis is a best practice. A wizard not only prompts for all costs to ensure conservatism, but it can tabulate costs in multiple currencies, a feature that is necessary for L&D organizations that are multinational in scope.

Figure 35: Cost Calculation Wizard for ROI Analysis

Cost Category Approach

Please enter your total costs related to each of these cost categories. If certain categories are not applicable, leave them blank. Please read **instructions for determining costs** to guide you in appropriately determining these numbers.

Your default currency is set to_____. To use a currency other than the default, use the drop-down box below. **NOTE:** This will only apply to this event.

Choose Your Currency: | USD—United States Dollars ▾ |

1) Tuition Costs: ?

The cost paid to external or internal learning providers to send participants through the program. | 0 |

2) Analysis Costs: ?

The cost of conducting a needs assessment prorated over the life of all programs for which it will be used. | 0 |

3) Development Costs: ?

The cost of designing and developing the program prorated over the life of all programs for which it will be used. | 0 |

4) Acquisition Costs: ?

The cost of purchased modules / segments to use directly or in a modified format prorated over the life of the program for which it will be used. | 0 |

5) Delivery Costs: ?

a. Facilitator salary, travel and equipment expenses, program materials and supplies, facilities costs: | 0 |

b. Participant Salary and Benefits: The cost of participant salaries and benefits for lost work time while attending the program. | 0 |

c. Participant travel, lodging and meals: | 0 |

6) Evaluation Costs: ?

The cost to evaluate and measure the program results. | 0 |

7) Overhead Costs: ?

Additional costs of the program not particularly related to the program (clerical support, departmental office expenses, etc.). | 0 |

Source: Metrics That Matter Learning Analytics Technology by KnowledgeAdvisors

A second ingredient of ROI Analysis is deriving and monetizing benefits. The Phillips ROI Process recommends action plans. Action plans are methods by which an L&D consultant gathers the business results data for program participants, isolates the impact of the data specific to the program, and applies the adjustment factors.

Figure 36 illustrates the results of an action plan exercise for a strategic program where multiple participants contributed to an action-planning exercise. Each participant's annual improvement for their specific results accruing from the program is stated and the isolation (contribution from the program) and confidence (adjustment factor) are computed to arrive at the adjusted value. This makes tabulating and monetizing results more methodological and process-oriented versus ad hoc and inconsistent.

Figure 36: Action Plan Tabulated Results

Phillips ROI Score Card summary results using the Phillips ROI Methodology

The current scale is 7. Numbers at or close to 7 indicate optimal performance.

Currency used for this report: USD—United States Dollars

Post Program Follow Up Business Impact Table

Participant	Annual Improvement	Measure	Measure Definition	Contribution from Program (%)	Confidence Estimate (%)	Adjusted Value
Jeff	108,000.00	quality	error rates	90	80	77,760.00
Mary	80,000.00	better decision	more strategic and timely decisions	70	60	33,600.00

Source: Metrics That Matter Learning Analytics Technology by KnowledgeAdvisors

Finally, Estimation/Isolation/Adjustment does not need to be a one-off exercise. Building it into the measurement process can ensure that the right data is ready for ROI Analysis when needed. Research suggests that when managers make decisions, they use analysis to validate their gut instinct. If not done in a timely manner, the analysis will eventually diminish in value.

KnowledgeAdvisors suggests gathering data and building seamless processes to estimate/isolate/adjust in a real-time manner, both at the end of an intervention (post event) and in follow-up (when back on the job), and to derive similar data inputs for ROI Analysis from managers for the "expert" estimation as mentioned by Phillips.

Figure 37 illustrates the results of an estimation/isolation/adjustment query in the Metrics That Matter Learning Analytics technology. The final adjusted percent improvement due to training is the main variable used for ROI Analysis. Comparing the adjusted percent across key programs, clients, lines of business, learning deliveries, and training vendors can help in sharpening future resource allocations.

Figure 37: Estimation/Isolation/Adjustment

Job Performance Change	Post Event	Follow Up	Manager
Total percent improvement in performance, including training	35%	40%	25%
Training's contribution to improved performance	70%	55%	75%
Percent of work time requiring knowledge skills	45%	40%	25%
Percent improvement due to training	11%	9%	5%
Adjustment factor for confidence in estimations	65%	65%	65%
Adjusted percent improvement due to training	7%	6%	3%

Source: Metrics That Matter Learning Analytics Technology by KnowledgeAdvisors

Process for ROI Analysis

KnowledgeAdvisors suggests that every L&D organization create a set of organized steps to ensure an organized process for ROI Analysis.

At a high level, the following are some basic steps for ROI Analysis:

1. Identify strategic, visible, and costly programs where ROI Analysis is needed.
2. Derive a data collection plan that outlines the data inputs (cost and benefit) needed, when the data will be collected, and how.
3. Identify a central database for storage of the data (cost and benefit).
4. Where feasible, automate the processing of the raw data into total program costs and adjusted benefit data where benefits have been estimated/isolated/adjusted.
5. Compute financial ROI calculations for the program by computing an ROI percentage, a benefit-to-cost ratio, and a payback period ratio.
6. Review the ROI calculations (a) at end of program as a forecast, and (b) post program as a more accurate estimate. Forecasting can help in deciding whether to continue the program through the end and what adjustments to make during the course of the program.
7. Analyze ROI calculations by drilling down into data to pinpoint the profiles of high- and low-performing ROI programs. Drill down by:

a. Class
b. Course
c. Curricula
d. Instructor
e. Vendor
f. Learning delivery
g. Location of delivery
h. Attribute of the participant (years of service, job role, business unit, geographic location)

8. Prioritize where strategic, costly, visible programs should be expanded or contracted, or remain the same.

9. Where positive ROI does occur, use it as a validation point with stakeholders. Be careful not to compare against the ROI on traditional assets, as the ROI on human capital tends to be higher, making it an invalid comparison.

10. Continue to monitor and measure ROI to ensure allocation of resources where the benefit relative to cost is optimal.

Profit Impact Analysis

Most HR professionals are uncomfortable with financial analysis and therefore do not understand how to link L&D investments to the bottom line. At the same time, business executives regard bottom-line impact as the primary way to make decisions regarding investments. Consequently, there has been a significant communication gap between learning professionals and business executives.

Contrary to popular belief in the learning industry, it is possible to estimate the bottom-line impact of learning programs. Corporate finance professionals are accustomed to doing pro forma financial analysis of marketing, R&D, technology, and fixed-asset investments, and then communicating bottom-line estimates to business executives. The same analysis can and should be done more often with significant learning investments.

The following table illustrates how the Phillips guiding principle of Estimation, Isolation, and Adjustment can be considered with traditional pro forma analysis.

Figure 38: Profit Impact Worksheet

Profit Impact Worksheet

($ in millions)		Q106	Q206	Q306	Q406	Q107
Revenue						
(1) Revenue with Learning Program		$ 100	$ 105	$ 115	$ 125	$ 130
(2) Estimated Revenue without Learning Program		$ 100	$ 108	$ 115	$ 120	$ 125
(3) Confidence Level in Estimate		50%	50%	50%	50%	50%
(4) Estimated Change in Revenue due to Learning Program	((1-2)*3)	$ —	$ (1.5)	$ —	$ 2.5	$ 2.5
Expenses						
(5) Costs with Learning Program		$ 80	$ 90	$ 95	$ 100	$ 115
(6) Learning and Development Costs		$ 2	$ —	$ —	$ —	$ —
(7) Estimated Cost Reduction due to Learning Program		$ —	$ —	$ 1	$ 2	$ 2
(8) Confidence Level in Estimate		100%	100%	100%	60%	60%
(9) Estimated Change in Costs due to Learning Program	(6-(7*8))	$ 2.0	$ —	$ (1.0)	$ (1.2)	$ (1.2)
Earnings						
(10) Earnings with Learning Program	(1-5)	$ 20	$ 15	$ 20	$ 25	$ 15
(11) Estimated Earnings without Learning Program	((1-4)-(5-9))	$ 22	$ 17	$ 19	$ 21	$ 11
(12) Estimated Earnings Impact due to Learning Program	(10-11)	$ (2.0)	$ (1.5)	$ 1.0	$ 3.7	$ 3.7
Profit Margin						
Estimated Change in Profit Margin due to Learning Program	(12/(1-4)	-2.00%	-1.41%	0.87%	3.02%	2.90%

Source: KnowledgeAdvisors

Since most business executives manage profit and loss statements, it is worth pursuing this type of analysis rather than simply saying you cannot link learning to earnings. Clearly it can be done.

Figure 39 shows another form of profit impact analysis. It illustrates how L&D managers can use the analysis to forecast future years' investments with and without proper L&D investments.

Figure 39. Profit Impact

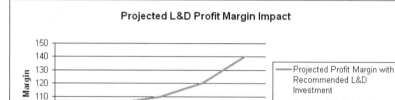

Source: KnowledgeAdvisors Profit Impact Analysis Template

Process for Profit Impact Analysis

KnowledgeAdvisors suggests that every L&D organization create a set of organized steps to ensure an organized process for Profit Impact Analysis.

At a high level, the following are some basic process steps for Profit Impact Analysis:

1. Create a template to house the key data inputs for profit impact analysis, including revenue, cost, earnings, and profit margin.
2. If you do not have financial analysis expertise, find someone in your organization or a third-party expert to help do the analysis.
3. Derive a baseline bottom-line impact analysis based on conservative assumptions.
4. Through sensitivity analysis, determine the optimal L&D investment to achieve the desired financial performance. Use this as a benchmark to determine if L&D is too high, too low, or on track to support revenue and human capital expenses (payroll).

VI. Overview of Learning Analytics and Measurement Models

We have discussed learning analytics but have yet to truly define it. This chapter will focus on what learning analytics is, and what its components are.

Learning analytics is the term used to describe the metrics that help organizations understand how to better train and develop employees, partners, and customers. There are four primary data sources that drive learning analytics. Figure 40 illustrates these data sources.

Figure 40: Data Sources Model

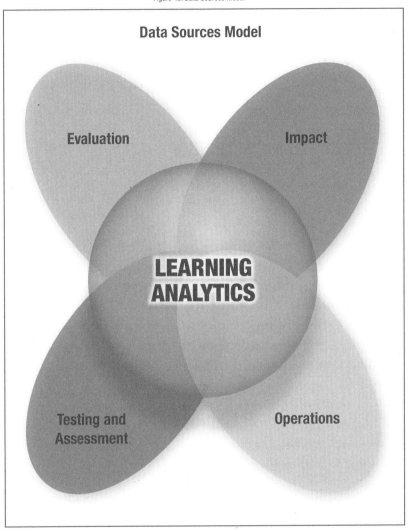

Of the four data sources, operations data is the most traditional data we know about today. This data is more activity- or volume-based and gives us information around how much we've trained. Examples of this type of data include the following:

- Enrollments
- Cancellations
- Completions
- Students trained
- Classes run

A primary source for this information is a learning management system (LMS). However, a typical LMS does a poor job of reporting this type of data and, more importantly, allowing the user to analyze the data in the desired fashion. Therefore, learning analytics tools can receive imports from the LMS on this data to then analyze self-sufficiently.

Figure 41 shows an example of an analytics tool, Metrics That Matter that has been fed data and now reports the results. In this case, it is basic activity sorted by instructor.

Figure 41: Basic Activity Data by Instructor

Activity Analytics

Indicators of the volume elements of training (i.e. how much training occured)

Basic Data by Instructor

Time Period for Reporting: Aug 1, 2004 to Aug 31, 2004

	Enrolled	No. of Locations	No. of Instructors	No. of Learning Providers	No. of Clients	No. of Courses
Brach, Merrie	9	1	1	1	1	2
Shah, Divyesh	7	1	1	1	3	2
Smith, Adam	41	1	1	1	2	1

	No. of Instructor Led Classes
Brach, Merrie	2
Shah, Divyesh	2
Smith, Adam	1

	No. of Post Event Evals	No. of Follow Up Evals
Brach, Merrie	9	0
Shah, Divyesh	3	0
Smith, Adam	37	22

Custom Query Criteria report limited by the following categories:

Reporting Date: Aug 1, 2004 to Aug 31, 2004

Source: KnowledgeAdvisors Metrics That Matter Learning Analytics Technology

Testing and assessment data is the next type of
analytic data. This data looks at business or
organizational needs data, competency data, and pre-
or post-test data, all of which are important.

A typical organizational- or business-needs
assessment is optimized if it gathers, by business unit,
the perception of business managers as to where the
business is going in the next 12, 24, or 36 months
regarding the below data items:

- Business results (e.g., sales, quality,
  cycle time)
- Business processes / initiatives (e.g.,
  finance and accounting, procurement,
  information technology)
- Competencies (e.g., conflict resolution,
  business acumen)
- Internal drivers (e.g., people, process,
  technology, culture)
- External drivers (e.g., economy,
  regulations)

A great example of a business assessment is the case
of a major consumer packaged-goods company.
Their L& D group would normally send an e-mail
with four questions to the business owners once every
twenty-four months. Data back was ad hoc and not
easy to analyze. Leveraging the above-mentioned
tool, the company was able to add structure and
meaning to their assessment.

Talent management relies heavily on competency management assessment. Standard competencies that should apply across the employee base and be measured and analyzed in your learning analytics include the following:

- Conflict management
- Continual learning
- Creativity/innovation
- Customer service
- Decisiveness
- Entrepreneurship
- External awareness
- Financial management
- Flexibility
- HR management
- Negotiating
- Integrity
- Interpersonal skills
- Diversity
- Communications
- Political savvy
- Project management resilience
- Self-direction
- Self-motivation
- Strategic thinking
- Team building
- Technical credibility
- Technology management
- Vision
- Analytical thinking

A great example of competency management is the case of a department within the federal government of the United States. After attempting to use a slick competency management tool, the department needed simplicity. They leveraged a standard instrument like the above and quickly got data back regarding thousands of employees. This data was then filtered by agency within the department. Those who completed the tool got immediate guidance and links to L&D resources, where they rated themselves weak on certain competencies.

Testing data is also important to understand where knowledge transfer and learning effectiveness occur and where certifications can be granted. The key to good testing tools, where resources are limited, is simplicity. Below are some simplicity guidelines:

- Multichoice / 1 answer
- One point each
- Mass settings to randomize or use validation
- Easy to add a logo, renumber, make edits
- Easy to author guidance to respondents if their score is low

A great example of test data is the case of an insurance company that was trying to build an auto liability learning program. Prior to design, they leveraged a testing tool and built forty scenarios. The scenarios were given to a sample of the population that would ultimately receive training. Based on the results, the company knew where to focus the design and what types of personnel needed basic or advanced versions of the program.

Another data source is evaluation data. Evaluation data is the most likely area where change can occur with little resistance and few resources. This is because almost all L&D organizations do evaluation. Maybe it is a smile sheet at the end of class, but it is an evaluation. The goal is to give more meaning to those data collection points, which are a natural point in the process.

There are four primary types of evaluation that can be deployed. If standardized across the organization and if technology automates the collection, processing, and storage of data, they can be powerful.

The first type of evaluation is a pre-event evaluation. This is a simple form that goes to the participant (and the manager who is preparing the participant for learning). It asks about expectations, current skills, and more importantly, whether they've talked about how they will use the learning once back on the job so as to optimize the impact. It is an excellent tool to lower any barrier to impact.

Another type of evaluation is a post-event evaluation. This is the end-of-class survey. However, we do not suggest that this be a smile sheet. It should incorporate a balanced set of measures that measure quality or satisfaction and effectiveness, predict impact, link to business results, and calculate a financial ROI. We will cover this later in the book.

The next type of evaluation is a follow-up evaluation. This true's up any predicted impact, results, and ROI forecasts from the post event and is typically administered 60 to 90 days later. The key is to look at this data for any evidence of "scrap learning." Scrap learning means that the learning was not applied at all or only minimally. Asking for this data as well as the reasons for low or no application is important in order to reduce scrap or wasted learning. Believe it or not, there is a 45 to 55% scrap rate in learning (based on analysis of KnowledgeAdvisors' benchmark database), and some say it is much higher.

Finally, a manager evaluation can be pushed out at the same time the learner does the follow-up. This evaluation is similar to the learner's follow-up, but is from the manager's perspective.

If over surveying is an issue, be selective. Focus on certain courses where human capital performance is expected to improve and forego it for the regulatory trainees or page-turners where performance was not meant to be improved.

However, optimize response rates. Reminder messages are great tools in this regard, and technology can automate the distribution. However, the biggest bang comes from the change in process. We suggest an Evaluation Notification. This is presented by the instructor when announcing the course objectives and thoroughly addresses when, why, how, and what the evaluation is all about. It is mentioned at least two more times before the students leave. Reminder messages will yield higher response rates. Figure 42 is a sample evaluation notice.

Figure 42. Sample Evaluation Notice

Sample Evaluation Notice

Training Evaluation Notice

Thank you for attending training. Your candid and objective feedback is important to us. We use this information to improve the training and ensure it is effective on your job. Below is some information on the evaluation process.

Why?
Because your feedback is extremely important and because we run training like a business and this provides critical operational feedback. We need this information not only to improve our processes but to have a meaningful discussion with your management on the value of the training to your business and job function.

What?
The evaluation is taken very seriously by our organization. It has elements of your satisfaction. In addition, it collects your opinion on learning effectiveness. Most importantly, it provides your management and ours with information on the impact it will have on the job and business results.

When?
An electronic evaluation will be e-mailed to you following this training. It will take no more that 2 minutes to complete and it will help us in understanding your satisfaction and the training's perceived value if you complete it within 48 hours of receiving it.

How?
You will complete the survey electronically. Simply click on the link or copy/paste it into your browser and begin to complete the information we request. Again, this is critical to our understanding the impact of the training on your job.

Follow-Up Evaluation
Approximately two months (60 days) after the end date of a class, you will receive a Follow-Up Evaluation. This brief survey will focus on if and when you applied the training to your job. This evaluation is critical to understanding the effect of the training in practice. We would appreciate 60 seconds of your time in completing it as well.

Thank you again for your time in attending the training and your consideration in completing this important evaluation.

Learning & Development Team

Source: KnowledgeAdvisors

If you do it right, you can optimize response rates. However, Figure 43 has some norms for response rates, depending on your delivery mechanism.

Figure 43: Response Rate Norms

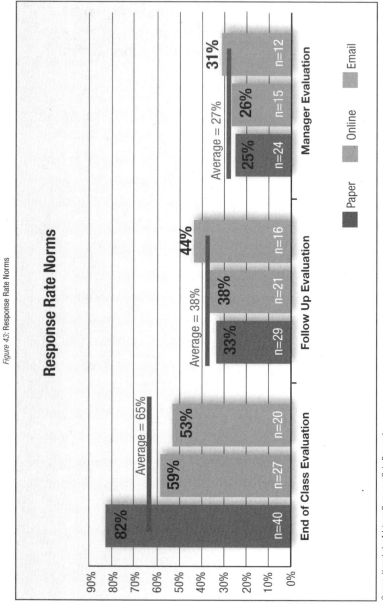

Response Rate Norms

End of Class Evaluation

82% (n=40)
59% (n=27)
53% (n=20)
Average = 65%

Follow Up Evaluation

33% (n=29)
38% (n=21)
44% (n=16)
Average = 38%

Manager Evaluation

25% (n=24)
26% (n=15)
31% (n=12)
Average = 27%

■ Paper   ■ Online   ■ Email

Source: KnowledgeAdvisors Response Rate Research

The final component of analytics is impact data. Impact data comes in two forms: at the program level and at the overall L&D level. Impact data are the changes that are the result of learning. It is your true performance data. Impact data is the toughest to obtain but the most compelling if you can get it.

At the program level we will discuss tools that can be used to gather evidence of impact. A great way to do this is by conducting an impact study, and the best way to do that is by deploying the Phillips ROI Process. That process attempts to look at each learning level in the Kirkpatrick Learning Levels Model by building a business process to measure those levels and by adding a financial ROI component.

Before going further, it is important to explain the Kirkpatrick Model and how the Phillips ROI Process ties into it. In 1959, Donald L. Kirkpatrick, author, PhD, consultant, past president of the ASTD and KnowledgeAdvisors Advisory Board member, published a series of four articles called "Techniques for Evaluating Training Programs." The articles described the four levels of evaluation that he had formulated based on his work for his PhD dissertation at the University of Wisconsin, Madison. Later, Kirkpatrick wrote a book (Donald L. Kirkpatrick, *Evaluating Training Programs: The Four Levels*, Berrett-Koehler Publishers, Inc., San Francisco, 1998) and it is now in its second edition. This book was a source for the information on the following pages relating to Levels One through Four.

Kirkpatrick's goal was to clarify the meaning of evaluation. The model defined evaluation as "measuring changes in behavior that occur as a result of training programs."

The model itself is composed of four levels of training evaluation. A fifth level, ROI, has been added since then. The fifth level was the brainchild of Dr. Jack J. Phillips, PhD. author, consultant, and KnowledgeAdvisors Advisory Board member and strategic partner.

Below is a narrative for each level.

Level One — Reaction
Per Kirkpatrick, "Evaluating reaction is the same thing as measuring customer satisfaction. If training is going to be effective, it is important that students react favorably to it."

The guidelines for Level One are as follows:
♦ Determine what you want to find out
♦ Design a form that will quantify the reactions
♦ Encourage written comments and suggestions
♦ Strive for 100% immediate response
♦ Get honest responses
♦ Develop acceptable standards
♦ Measure reactions against standards, and take appropriate action
♦ Communicate reactions as appropriate

The benefits to conducting Level One Evaluations are:

- A proxy for customer satisfaction
- Immediate and real-time feedback to an investment
- A mechanism to measure and manage learning providers, instructors, courses, locations, and learning methodologies
- A way to control costs and strategically spend your budget dollars
- If done properly, a way to gauge a perceived return on learning investment

Level Two – Learning
Level Two is a "test" to determine if the learning transfer occurred. Per Kirkpatrick, "It is important to measure learning because no change in behavior can be expected unless one or more of these learning objectives have been accomplished. Measuring learning means determining one or more of the following":

- What knowledge was learned?
- What skills were developed or improved?
- What attitudes were changed?

The guidelines for Level Two are as follows:
- Use a control group, if practical
- Evaluate knowledge, skills, and/or attitudes both before and after the program
- Use a "test" to measure knowledge and attitudes
- Strive for 100% response
- Use the results to take corrective actions

The benefits to conducting Level Two Evaluations are:

- Learner must demonstrate the learning transfer
- Training managers receive more conclusive evidence of training effectiveness

Level Three — Behavior

Level Three evaluates the job impact of training. Per Kirkpatrick, "What happens when trainees leave the classroom and return to their jobs? How much transfer of knowledge, skill, and attitudes occurs? In other words, what change in job behavior occurred because people attended a training program?"

The guidelines for Level Three are as follows:

- Use a control group, if practical
- Allow time for behavior change to take place
- Evaluate both before and after the program, if practical
- Survey or interview trainees, supervisors, subordinates, and others who observe their behavior
- Strive for 100% response
- Repeat the evaluation at appropriate times

The benefits to conducting Level Three Evaluations are as follows:

- An indication of the "time to job impact"
- An indication of the types of job impacts occurring (cost, quality, time, productivity)

Level Four — Results

Per Kirkpatrick, Level Four is "the most important step and perhaps the most difficult of all." Level Four attempts to look at the business results that accrued because of the training.

The guidelines for Level Four are as follows:
- Use a control group, if practical
- Allow time for results to be achieved
- Measure both before and after the program, if practical
- Repeat the measurement at appropriate times
- Consider costs versus benefits
- Be satisfied with evidence if proof not possible

The benefits to conducting Level Four evaluations. are as follows:
- Determine bottom-line impact of training
- Tie business objectives and goals to training

Level Five — ROI

Level Five is not a Kirkpatrick step. Kirkpatrick alluded to ROI when he created Level Four, linking training results to business results. However, over time the need to measure the dollar-value impact of training became so important to corporations that a fifth level was added by Dr. Phillips. Dr. Phillips outlines his approach to Level Five in his book *Return on Investment in Training and Performance Improvement Programs*, Butterworth Heinemann, Publishers, Inc, Woburn, MA 1997. Dr. Phillips has written extensively on the subject, publishing or editing dozens of books on the topic of ROI.

The guidelines for Level Five are as follows:

- Use a control group, if practical
- Allow time for results to be achieved
- Determine the direct costs of the training
- Measure productivity or performance both before and after the training
- Measure the productivity or performance increase
- Translate the increase into a dollar-value benefit
- Subtract the dollar-value benefit from the cost of training
- Calculate the ROI

ROI calculations are being done by a few world-class training organizations. They help these organizations to:

- Quantify the performance improvements
- Quantify the dollar-value benefits
- Compute investment returns
- Make informed decisions based on quantified benefits, returns, and percent return comparisons between learning programs

Dr. Phillips has created an ROI Methodology™ and conducts certifications and workshops on it, and has helped training organizations use the right tools to measure the ROI on organizational learning. A summary of his methodology is illustrated below:

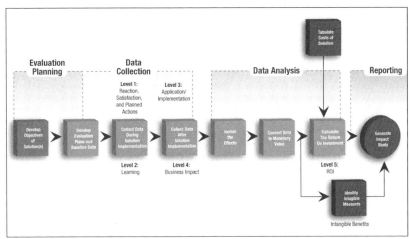

Source: Measuring the Return on Investment in Training and Development Certification Materials, Jack J. Phillips, PhD, 2002

Dr. Phillips's methodology is a comprehensive approach to training measurement. It begins with planning the project (which Dr. Phillips calls an "impact study"). It moves into the tools and techniques to collect data, analyze the data, and finally report the data. The result is not only a Level 5 ROI but also measurements on the Kirkpatrick 4 Levels as well. This yields a balanced scorecard approach to the measurement exercise.

Accepted methods of gathering impact data can be achieved through the Phillips ROI Process. A key principle of this process is to estimate, isolate and adjust. There are many ways to isolate the effects of learning impact. These are as follows:

Control Group Analysis — this is beneficial when the control group is naturally occurring and homogeneous. If you can show evidence that the trained group had a more favorable impact than the control group that isolates in a reasonable manner to the training.

Trend Analysis — review of data before the learning and after. If the data shows a positive trend, then it is reasonable to conclude that the learning made an impact. The problem is, it takes time to build the trends and management wants the data sooner rather than later in order to make decisions. Management cannot wait for trends to emerge.

Statistical Analysis — review of actual results data and comparison of this data to the training taken by individuals generating those results. Does the data show that existence of certain training yielded better results and is statistically valid? If so, that is evidence of impact. The problem here is getting your hands on the clean data to analyze it in a timely manner. Often, it is not clean or clear or timely.

The final isolation method is participant or expert estimation. Using this method, you ask people to estimate the change in a result, isolate it to learning, and apply an adjustment factor due to the subjectivity of the method. This is a frequently used approach because the other approaches pose challenges, but it is less precise, hence the adjustment factor.

Here is an example of this approach:

Step One: Estimate the change in the business result(s).

(A) In the coming months, given all factors, how much do you estimate you will improve upon specific business objectives related to the subject matter of this training? (e.g., increased productivity, decreased costs)? — a Level 4 question

☐0% ☐10% ☐20% ☐30% ☐40% ☐50% ☐60% ☐70% ☐80% ☐90% ☐100%

Example: 30%

Step Two: Isolate the estimated improvement specifically to training.

(B) Based on your response to the prior question, estimate how much of this improvement will be a direct result of this training. For example, if half of your estimated increase in productivity or quality was specifically due to the training, you would input 50% here.

☐0% ☐10% ☐20% ☐30% ☐40% ☐50% ☐60% ☐70% ☐80% ☐90% ☐100%

Example: 20%

Step Three: Calculate benefit.

A x B = C
C=benefit

Example: .30 x .20 = .06

Step Four: Obtain a confidence interval and adjust benefit.

For the percentage estimations you provided above, how confident were you in placing those estimates? (0% is no confidence, 100% is complete confidence)

☐0% ☐10% ☐20% ☐30% ☐40% ☐50% ☐60% ☐70% ☐80% ☐90% ☐100%

Example: 60%

C x D = E
D = confidence internal, E = adjusted benefit

Example: .06x.60 = .036 or 3.6%

Step Five: Monetize the benefit.

Use the average salary as the monetization factor and multiply by the benefit.

Example: Salary

Example: .036 x $40,000

Assume $40,000 is average salary = $1,440 monetized benefit.

Step 6: Subtract the costs.

Determine the cost of training and subtract it from the benefit to yield an ROI.

Example: Cost is $1,000 and benefit was $1,440. ROI is $440.

Step 7: Calculate a benefit-to-cost ratio

$1440/$1000 = 1.44 (i.e., the training returns 1.44 dollars for every dollar invested)

Besides the impact of a particular program, there is the power of tracking actual business results. This, too, is impact data. Tracking the actual results and looking at their direction over time or against goals is a great way to keep a pulse on business impact. We will discuss this further in later chapters. However, never underestimate the power of tracking the following types of data and, as a leader in learning, being able to have a seat at the table by understanding these trends to help the business improve performance:

1. Error rates
2. Customer satisfaction rates
3. Revenue
4. Productivity (revenue/employees)
5. Operating profit
6. Cycle time

VII. Presenting a Measurement Method That Is Practical and Scalable

No matter how robust a measurement strategy is, if the process to execute the strategy is not one that fits the financial, physical, and human resource limitations, it will not likely succeed. This chapter suggests ways in which organizations can live within limitations but still have a constant flow of robust learning measurement data to help with information decision making.

It is important to begin with the challenges. Within your organization, start by listing the potential barriers to your success. In learning measurement and evaluation, the most common challenges are as follows:

- Global training operations
- Limited data collection from participants
- Huge volumes of students, classes, locations, etc.
- Timeliness — receiving the metrics in time to make decisions is a critical requirement
- Scalability and flexibility of the process in place
- Consistency across the organization for aggregate analysis
- Meeting needs of multiple stakeholders within and outside of learning and development
- Following requirements by third parties, internal customers, and management
- Implementing limited financial, physical, and human resources in the measurement process

Bearing in mind the above challenges, you can begin to examine your own measurement process in order to determine where the largest gaps are for continuous improvement. As you take each of these steps, ask the following questions:

- Can we apply a template so as not to have redundant and provide guidance in practice?

- Can we leverage automation or technology to reduce administrative burden and risk of error?

- Can we create a standard that can apply across the organization so as to have consistent and reliable information that can be trended and aggregated in the future?

There are four primary steps in the learning measurement process (you may wish to compare them to your own):

Step 1: Data Collection. Data from other systems, participants, managers, tests, etc. must be collected, which involves doing the following:
- Define the metrics you desire for reporting and analysis.
- Design the instruments (standards and templates) to retrieve the underlying data.
- Determine the population you desire to collect this data from, and ensure that collection will be secure and reliable.

- Disseminate instruments, leveraging technology as much as possible.
- Collect data by being flexible to the limitations that may exist (paper vs. online collection).

Step 2: Data Storage. Your ultimate goal is to ensure one central repository for all of your data, which involves doing the following:

- Design a database that is flexible and able to handle the volume of data within your organization.
- Store data in a central location so that processing (the next step) can begin from a single point.
- Ensure that data entry (from the previous step) has as few handoffs to get to the database as possible.
- Ensure that data is secure (review data privacy and protection laws and internal management policies).
- Ensure access to raw data.

Step 3: Data Processing. The goal here is to leverage technologies that allow for self-sufficiency in manipulating data to meet a variety of needs. This involves doing the following:

- Ensure that data flows from a single repository.
- Consider building preset queries or, more logically, implement an OLAP (online analytical processing) engine to

allow for slicing and dicing of data in a user-friendly interface.

- Convert data into metrics. L&D managers should have defined the metrics in the first phase so that the queries can now be written or users can self-sufficiently process raw data to yield those metrics.

Step 4: Data reporting. The metrics should now be available in a tabular or graphical format ready for analysis. This involves doing the following:

- Create standard reports that meet 80% of the needs. These canned reports avoid multiple requests and redundant work.
- Allow for self-sufficient ad hoc querying for the 20% of the time when a custom analysis is needed. Using the OLAP processing of the prior step will result in these reports.
- Ensure that data can be trended over time in reporting, a key step in analysis.
- Ensure that data can be compared internally and externally, a key step in analysis.
- Ensure that a user can "drill down" when needed to see the transaction level data.
- Design certain reports for management. We will discuss dashboards in a later chapter.

- Make it a habit to review a summary report (ideally, on a quarterly basis) with management to keep metrics top of mind.

It is important to note that these four steps are administrative in nature. They "ready" data for analysis. No analysis or decisions are made in these steps. KnowledgeAdvisors research shows that over 81% of an L&D resource investment in measurement is tied up in "readying" data. That leaves less than a fifth of time to do something with the data, such as improve future programs or validate to management the programs you've run.

The goal is to ask the questions around templates, standards, and technology. Pulling these levers in the collection, storage, processing, and reporting steps can cut significant amounts of administration out of the measurement process. This will free up time for using the information for decision making.

Let's talk about templates. Templates are pre-created tools that allow a user to input or import data so there is less risk of error or inconsistency. Probably the biggest area of focus for L&D from a template perspective is the up-front planning process in which L&D attempts to link a future learning investment to a customer business result. Without a consultative tool to walk through this process, L&D may end up consuming the entire business result as its own.

Figure 44 shows a template that can be used by L&D managers in this process.

Figure 44: Analyst Worksheet to Link Learning and Results

Sales Training Worksheet - Analyst Results Report
Summary of comprehensive business impact and ROI analysis

Business Result: Increased Sales
Defined as: Closed Slaes per Year

Change in Metric	Group Trained		Control Group	
	Metric	Monetary Value	Metric	Monetary Value
Metric BEFORE Training	45	$90,000	45	$90,000
Metric AFTER Training	70	$140,000	48	$96,000
Percent Change	56%	$50,000	7%	$6,000

Root Cause of Change

	Group Trained		Control Group	
	Metric	Monetary Value	Metric	Monetary Value
Personal	15%	$7,500	12%	$720
Technology	0%	$0	0%	$0
External Factors	15%	$7,500	30%	$1,800
Procedure Policy	5%	$2,500	5%	$300
Incentives	10%	$5,000	15%	$900
Training	55%	$27,500	0%	$0
Other	0%	$0	38%	$2,280
Total	100%	$50,000	100%	$6,000

Adjustment in estimations	65%	
Business impact from training	20%	$17,875

Cost of training	$6,000
ROI of training	$11,875
Benefit to Cost Ratio	3
Payback Period in Months	4
ROI Percentage	197.9%

Source: KnowledgeAdvisors Metrics That Matter Learning Analytics Technology

The template allows the L&D manager to ask the right questions and to gather appropriate data to forecast the potential of a learning investment in a methodical and businesslike manner. At the end of the meeting, the output can show the actual benefit-to-cost analysis. If the program moves forward, this template can be referenced again at the end for a "true up" exercise based on the forecasted results.

Templates are guidelines. They avoid redundant work and help employees to be more productive in their roles.

Another important element of measurement is standards. The standard that may be the most challenging to obtain is a standard for evaluation. Evaluation is important because it is a scalable data collection tool and one that requires the least amount of change on behalf of learners, primarily because they have an expectation of it already within their learning process.

However, if standards are not applied, courses cannot be compared, business units cannot be compared, and aggregation of data is nearly impossible to do.

As a result, it is vital that the leaders of the analytics process collaborate with L&D managers to create a standard set of questions that can be applied across all programs, all the time. This is not to say that there can never be customization or program-specific data. However, ensuring that the standard is used will lead to a base set of robust data that can then be trended and benchmarked.

Figure 45 provides an example of an evaluation standard that KnowledgeAdvisors suggests and has used with hundreds of client on hundreds of thousands of learner evaluations.

Figure 45: Evaluation Standard for End of Event (Post- Event) Evaluation

'Reaction' Level 1

INSTRUCTOR

Strongly Agree — Strongly Disagree
7 6 5 4 3 2 1 n/a

1. The instructor was knowledgeable about the subject.
2. The instructor was prepared and organized for the class.
3. Participants were encouraged to take part in class discussions.
4. The instructor was responsive to participants' needs and questions.
5. The instructor's energy and enthusiasm kept the participants actively engaged.
6. On-the-job application of each object was discussed during the course.

ENVIRONMENT

Strongly Agree — Strongly Disagree
7 6 5 4 3 2 1 n/a

7. The physical environment was conducive to learning.

COURSEWARE

Strongly Agree — Strongly Disagree
7 6 5 4 3 2 1 n/a

8. The scope of the material was appropriate to meet my needs.
9. The material was organized logically.
10. The examples presented helped me understand the content.
11. The participant materials (manual, presentation handouts, etc.) will be useful on the job.

'Learning' Level 2

LEARNING EFFECTIVENESS

Strongly Agree — Strongly Disagree
7 6 5 4 3 2 1 n/a

12. I learned new knowledge and skills from this training.
13. Rate your INCREASE in skill level or knowledge of this content before versus after the training. A 0% is no increase and a 100% is a very significant increase.

0% 10% 20% 30% 40% 50% 60% 70% 80% 90% 100%

'Job Impact' Level 3

JOB IMPACT

Strongly Agree — Strongly Disagree
7 6 5 4 3 2 1 n/a

14. I will be able to apply the knowledge and skills learned in this class to my job.
15. What percent of your total work time requires the knowledge and skills presented in this training? Check only one.

0% 10% 20% 30% 40% 50% 60% 70% 80% 90% 100%

16. On a scale of 0% (not at all) to 100% (extremely critical), how critical is applying the content of this training to your job success? Check only one.

0% 10% 20% 30% 40% 50% 60% 70% 80% 90% 100%

'Results' Level 4 & Estimation Isolation Adjustment

JOB IMPACT

17. What percent of new knowledge and skills learned from this training do you estimate you will directly apply to your job? Check only one.

0% 10% 20% 30% 40% 50% 60% 70% 80% 90% 100%

BUSINESS RESULTS

Strongly Agree — Strongly Disagree
7 6 5 4 3 2 1 n/a

18. This training will improve my job performance.

19. Given all factors, including this training, estimate how much your job performance related to the course subject matter will improve.

0% 10% 20% 30% 40% 50% 60% 70% 80% 90% 100%

20. Based on your response to the prior question, estimate how much of the improvement will be a direct result of this training. (For example if you feel that half of your improvement is a direct result of the training, enter 60% here.)

0% 10% 20% 30% 40% 50% 60% 70% 80% 90% 100%

21. This training will have a significant impact on: (check all that apply)

- [ ] increasing quality
- [ ] increasing productivity
- [ ] increasing employee satisfaction
- [ ] increasing sales
- [ ] increasing customer satisfaction
- [ ] decreasing costs
- [ ] decreasing cycle time
- [ ] decreasing risk

RETURN ON INVESTMENT

Strongly Agree — Strongly Disagree
7 6 5 4 3 2 1 n/a

22. This training was a worthwhile investment in my career development.
23. This training was a worthwhile investment for my employer.

What about this class was *most* useful to you?

_____

What about this class was *least* useful to you?

_____

How can we improve the training to make it more relevant to your job?

_____

Would you like to be notified about advanced or complementary courses?
○ Yes   ○ No

'RO/ROE' Level 5

As you can see, the instrument is linked back to credible methodology from Donald Kirkpatrick and Jack Phillips. There are indicator constructs (question categories) and questions for each learning level. These are as follows:

Reaction/Level 1:
Instructor
Environment Courseware

Learning/Level 2:
Learning Effectiveness

Behavior/Level 3:
Job Impact

Results/Level 4:
Business Results

ROI/Level 5:
Return on Investment

The key is to devise a scalable and practical solution. It must apply globally and meet the diverse needs of multiple stakeholders without disrupting change. The instrument accomplishes all of these objectives:

This instrument:

- takes 2.5 minutes to complete, so it is not a burden on the learner
- can be translated into whatever local language is needed for a global audience

- meets the needs of many as it has elements of all learning levels
- is scalable as it can be used across all programs, therefore eliminating redundancies and lending itself to excellent aggregate capabilities

The instrument operates on the premise that one can gather perceptions to the Level 1 indicators. This is what training organizations have traditionally done, and it is referred to as a smile sheet or Level 1.

However, this instrument may be the only opportunity to collect good data. We need to leverage the opportunity for more than Level 1. Perhaps we don't have resources or the right environment for an empirical Level 2 or "test." We can use the Learning Effectiveness questions to gauge Level 2 if the questions are asked consistently and benchmarked over time and against other programs.

For example, a utility company asked the Level 2 indicator questions on their evaluations. They found that one program was lower than all the others. It prompted them to look into the program. The program was a local unit, post on boarding program. The participants underwent steps to climb utility poles. However, the local office was not aware that the central office in the main on boarding of new employees taught the same thing. Thus, the learning effectiveness scores the second time around were sharply lower. The metrics pinpointed this and the local program was modified. A "test" was not necessary to detect lack of learning. All that was needed was a question or two with comparisons. In addition, the evaluation will forecast or predict indicators of Levels 3, 4, and 5. These are then given better estimates when similar Follow-Up instruments have the same questions on them but from a past-tense perspective and can be given out on the job after a few months.

You can take it a step further and also distribute a supervisor form, using similar Level 3, 4, and 5 questions but from the manager perspective. The net result is that you can compare the Post-Event, Follow-Up and Manager data consistently during and after the program. The forecasts are just as valuable as the actual on-the-job evaluations because if your training significant numbers in between the Post Event Survey and the Follow-Up Survey.

The other factor for consideration in having a practical and scalable analytics process is leveraging of technology. This involves not only ensuring that technology at each step in the collection-store-process-and-report phase is optimized but also that any feeder systems can be integrated with analytics systems and databases.

Figure 46 shows a schematic of how a basic learning management system tool can interface with a learning analytics tool for evaluation and measurement.

Figure 46: Integration of LMS with Analytics Technologies

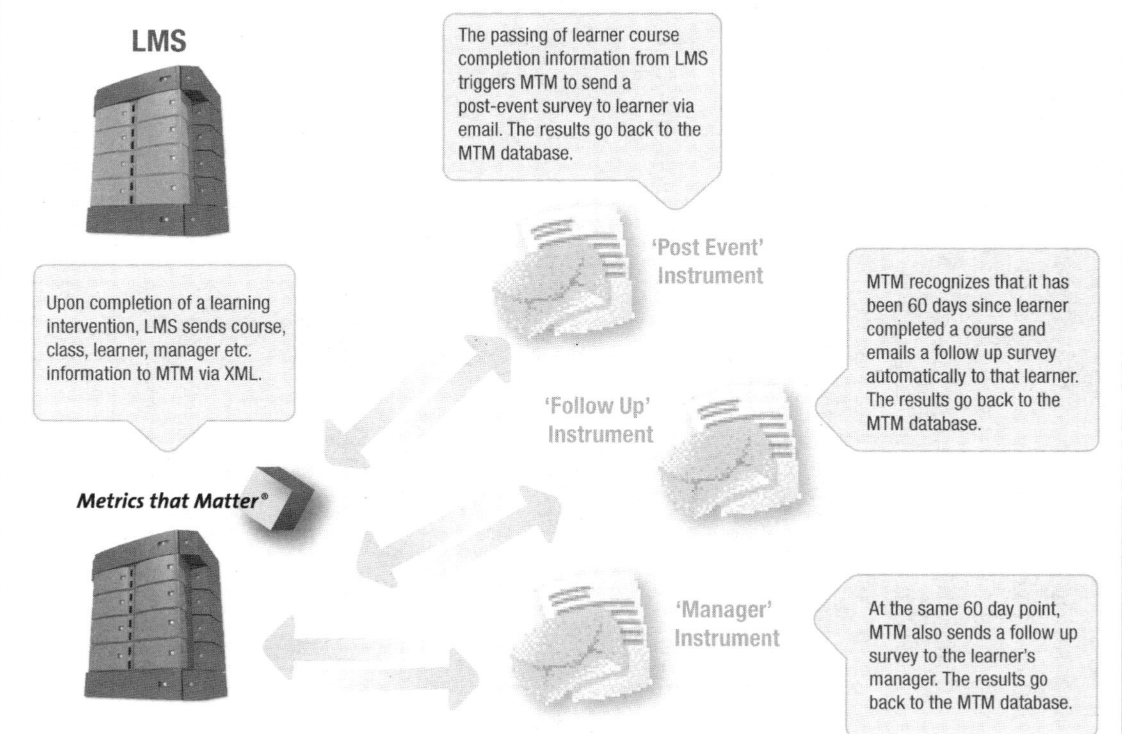

The passing of learner course completion information from LMS triggers MTM to send a post-event survey to learner via email. The results go back to the MTM database.

'Post Event' Instrument

MTM recognizes that it has been 60 days since learner completed a course and emails a follow up survey automatically to that learner. The results go back to the MTM database.

'Follow Up' Instrument

'Manager' Instrument

At the same 60 day point, MTM also sends a follow up survey to the learner's manager. The results go back to the MTM database.

LMS

Upon completion of a learning intervention, LMS sends course, class, learner, manager etc. information to MTM via XML.

Metrics that Matter®

Please Note: MTM can trigger follow-up and manager instruments to be sent out at anytime as defined by the customer. MTM results data can also be sent back to the LMS as required by the customer.

Source: KnowledgeAdvisors Integration Process

The schematic in Figure 46 assumes that the analytics technology is KnowledgeAdvisors' Metrics That Matter (MTM) system. However, any LMS (learning management system) should be able to interface with an analytics technology (like MTM) to pass relevant data from one system to another. The passing of basic class registration details to the analytics tool triggers a sequence of events in the analytics tool that starts the analytics process of collecting, storing, processing, and reporting data.

In terms of integrations, here are some additional details to know.

A solid analytics tool should be able to function as a stand-alone or integrated solution. Using Metrics That Matter (MTM) as an example, integrating MTM with your LMS or other class-scheduling database eliminates the data entry of class and student information into MTM. Additionally, it unlocks functionality that is not available in the manual solution.

There are four levels of MTM integration: Basic, Standard, Advanced, and Custom. Each progressive level provides additional types of information that can be imported. A description of each type and the drivers for selecting that type of integration are listed below.

BASIC INTEGRATION
Description: Import basic class information (course, instructor, date, etc.).

Drivers: Eliminate manual data entry in MTM and synchronize LMS and MTM data.

STANDARD INTEGRATION
Description: Import basic class information, along with students and multiple training providers.
Drivers: Automate the delivery of survey invitation e-mails. Import student demographics (job type, department, etc.) from your LMS. If you have more than one MTM account, the standard integration allows you to import classes to each of your organizations.

ADVANCED INTEGRATION
Description: The standard integration, plus enrollment updates and survey assignments by class.
Drivers: Pass updates and cancellations to student enrollments to enhance the metrics in activity-based reports in MTM. Assign surveys at the class level, which can be useful for multi-language support and more complex survey assignment logic.

CUSTOM INTEGRATION
Description: All fields can be passed, including curriculum hierarchies and evaluation answer data.
Drivers: Group courses into programs by importing curriculum hierarchies. Import evaluation answer data from an existing database into MTM.

The following table summarizes the integration details mentioned above.

Figure 47. Integration Summary

Available Fields	Basic	Standard	Advanced	Custom
Course	•	•	•	•
Instructor	•	•	•	•
Location	•	•	•	•
Class	•	•	•	•
Training Organization		•	•	•
Student		•	•	•
Enrollment Updates			•	•
Survey			•	•
Curriculum Hierarchy				•
Answer Data				•

Source: MTM integration overview

At the end of the day, build a process that leverages standards, templates, and technology. To the extent that can be done, you will be able to scale your process and reduce administrative burden.

VIII. Valuation Models for Deriving Impact, Results, and ROI

In this chapter we will explore three models for calculating impact, results, and ROI. We will go through the main benefits of each approach and when to apply them, walk through the mechanics of the models, and present real-world examples of how they were used in practice.

Figure 48 illustrates the three models we will be discussing and summarizes their main features.

Figure 48: Valuation Models

Cost and Complexity

Human Capital
① ② ③ ④ ⑤

Focus on Level 3—Job Impact

- Indicators on all 5 Learning Levels in Kirkpatrick/Phillips models with a focus on Level 3
- A job impact financial ROI computed
- Very scalable and replicable
- Easy for participants to complete
- Solid indicator of ROI on performance relative to the individuals Human Capital (i.e. salary)
- Leverage Phillips principles of estimation, isolation, and adjustment
- Use 100% of the time

Business Result
① ② ③ ④ ⑤

Focus on Level 4—Results

- Indicators on all 5 Learning Levels in Kirkpatrick/Phillips model with a focus on Level 4
- An ROI relative to specific business results
- Practical if leverage technology
- More complex for participants to complete
- Leverages Phillips principles of estimation, isolation, and adjustment
- Could be used 100% of the time or on a case by case basis

Impact Study Process
① ② ③ ④ ⑤

Focus on Level 5—ROI

- Indicators on all 5 Learning levels in Kirkpatrick/Phillips model with a focus on Level 5
- A formalized process for conducting in depth ROI impact studies
- Rigorous approach
- Technology facilitates tasks
- Requires serious investments of participant time
- Authored by Drs. Jack and Patti Phillips leveraging all components of their ROI process
- Suggested to be used 5 to 10% of the time

Source: KnowledgeAdvisors ROI Models white paper

Before we go into further detail on these models, let's start with something easier: the cost side of the valuation equation. Costs of an L&D initiative need to be conservative in order to make the final valuation credible.

There are seven major categories of cost you should consider for L&D investment valuation. These costs are as follows:

1. Tuition. Costs paid to external or internal learning providers to send participants through the program.

2. Analysis. Cost of conducting a needs assessment prorated over the life of all programs for which it will be used.

3. Development. Cost of designing and developing the program prorated over the life of all programs for which it will be used.

4. Acquisition. Cost of purchased modules/segments to use directly or in a modified format prorated over the life of the program for which it will be used.

5. Delivery. Costs composed of the following:

   a. Facilitator salary, travel expenses, program materials and supplies, facilities costs, equipment expenses

  b. Participant salary and benefits (cost of participant salaries and benefits for lost work time while attending the program)

  c. Participant travel, lodging, and meals

 6. Evaluation. Cost to evaluate and measure the program results.

 7. Overhead. Additional costs of the program not specifically related to the program — for example, clerical support, departmental office expenses etc.

There are even more details behind each of these cost categories. Because of this, we suggest a cost calculation template for each initiative that requires a deep cost analysis. Figure 49 illustrates the components of the template.

Figure 49. Cost Calculation Template

PHYSICAL COUNTS:
This brief section is meant to help us understand number of people who went through the program being evaluated by this measurement study.

1. **How many participants attended the program being evaluated?** [   ]

TUITION COSTS:

1. Participant 'tuition.'
(Number of participants x cost per participant to attend the program. This cost may exist if you charge/incur a fee for employees to attend internal training or paid a fee for employees to go to training provided by a third party.) [   ]

ANALYSIS COSTS:
One of the most often overlooked items is the cost of conducting a needs assessment. In some programs this cost is zero because the program is conducted without a needs assessment. However, as more organizations focus increased attention on needs assessment, this item will become a more significant cost in the future. All costs associated with the needs assessment should be captured to the fullest extent possible. These costs include the time of staff members conducting the assessment, direct fees and expenses for external consultants who conduct the needs assessment, and internal services and supplies used in the analysis. The total costs are usually prorated over the life of the program. Depending on the type and nature of the program, the shelf life should be kept to a very reasonable number in the one- to two-year timeframe. Of course the exception would be very expensive programs that are not expected to change significantly for several years.

NOTE: If you incurred a 1 time 'tuition' cost for training and do not have analysis costs, please refer to the section 'Tuition Costs' where Tuition can be input.

1. **What is the estimated number of months between the original needs assessment and when another assessment is required?** [   ]

2. **How many total participants do you expect to participate in the program during the months indicated above?** [   ]

3. **What is the total cost of conducting a needs assessment prior to the creation or purchase of the program?** [   ]
    (Consider in your total cost estimate salaries and benefits of those conducting the needs assessment, direct expenses, payments to outside vendors)

4. **Total Prorated Analysis costs.** [   ]
    (Question 3/ Question 2) x Question 1 under the Physical Counts Category

DEVELOPMENT COSTS:
One of the more significant items is the cost of designing and developing the program. These costs include internal staff time in both design and development and the purchase of supplies, videos, CD ROMs, and other material directly related to the program. It would also include the use of consultants. As with needs assessment costs, design and development costs are usually prorated, perhaps using the same timeframe. One to two years is recommended unless the program is not expected to change for many years and the costs are significant.

NOTE: If you incurred a 1 time 'tuition' cost for training and do not have development costs, please refer to the section 'Tuition Costs' where Tuition can be input.

1. **What is the estimated number of months between the original development and when a major re-development is required?**

2. **How many total participants do you expect to participate in the program during the months indicated above?**

3. **Salaries and employee benefits of staff involved in the development.**
(Number of people x average salary x employee benefits factor x number of hours on project.)

4. **Direct expenses**
(Consider in your total cost estimate salaries and benefits of those developing the program, direct expenses, payments to outside vendors.)

5. **Program materials and supplies - Total**

       a. **Web based tools**
       b. **Videotape**
       c. **Audiotapes**
       d. **Slides (Powerpoint, overheads)**
       e. **CD Rom**
       f. **Artwork**
       g. **Manuals and materials**
       h. **Other**

6. **External services**

7. **Total Development Costs**
(this is an automatic calculation of items 3-6)

ACQUISITION COSTS:

In lieu of development costs, many organizations purchase programs to use directly or in a modified format. The acquisition costs for these programs include the purchase price for the instructor materials, train-the-trainer sessions, licensing agreements, and other costs associated with the right to deliver the program. These acquisition costs should be prorated using the same rationale above; one to two years should be sufficient. If modification of the program is needed or some additional development is required, these costs should be included as development costs. In practice, many programs have both acquisition costs and development costs.

NOTE: If you incurred a 1 time 'tuition' cost for training and do not have acquisition costs, please refer to the section 'Tuition Costs' where Tuition can be input.

1. What is the estimated number of months between the original acquisition and when a major re-acquisition is required?

2. How many total participants do you expect to participate in the program during the months indicated above?

3. Purchase price for acquired instructor materials

4. Cost of train-the-trainer sessions.

5. Licensing or royalty costs associated with acquired materials

6. Other costs associated with the right to deliver the program

7. Total Acquisition Costs
   (this is an automatic calculation of items 3-6)

8. Total Prorated Acquisition Costs.
   (Question 7 / Question 2) x Question 1 under the Physical Counts Category

DELIVERY COSTS:

Usually the largest segment of training costs would be those associated with delivery. The nine major categories are listed below.

1. Participant salaries and benefits.

(Number of participants x average salary x employee benefits factor x hours or days of training time.)

2. Participant travel lodging and meals

(Direct travel for participants. Lodging and meals are included for participants during travel, as well as meals during the stay for the program. Refreshments should also be included. For estimates review participant surveys as they were asked to estimate this cost on their surveys. You can use this to then create a total cost estimate to be input here.)

3. Facilitator Salaries and benefits.

4. Facilitator travel lodging and meals

(Direct travel for facilitators and coordinators. Lodging and meals are included for facilitators and coordinators during travel, as well as meals during the stay for the program.)

5. Program materials and supplies

(Notebooks, textbooks, CD ROMs, case studies, exercises, and participant workbooks should be included in the delivery costs, along with license fees, user fees, and royalty payments. Pens, paper, certificates, calculators, and personal copies of software are also included in this category.)

6. Facilities Cost / Rental/ Expense Allocation

(The direct cost of the facilities should be included. For external programs, this is the direct charge from the conference center, hotel, or motel. If the program is conducted in-house, the conference room represents a cost for the organization, and the cost should be estimated and included even if it is not the practice to include facilities' cost in other reports. The cost of internal facilities can easily be estimated by obtaining a room rental rate of a similar size room at a local hotel. Sometimes this figure is available on a square foot basis from the Finance and Accounting staff, i.e., the actual value of the square footage on a daily basis. In other situations, the cost of commercial real estate on a square foot basis could be determined locally from commercial real estate directors or the newspaper. The important point is to quickly come to a very credible estimate for the value of the cost of the room. Refreshments should also be included.)

7. Equipment expenses

8. Other miscellaneous expenses

9. Total Delivery Costs

(this is an automatic calculation of items 1-8)

EVALUATION COSTS:

Usually the total evaluation cost is included in the program costs to compute the fully loaded cost. ROI costs include the cost of developing the evaluation strategy, designing instruments, collecting data, data analysis, and report preparation and distribution. Cost categories include time, materials, purchased instruments, or surveys. Estimates are acceptable.

1. What is the total cost of conducting the evaluation of the program to measure its results?

(Consider in your total cost estimate salaries and benefits of those conducting the evaluation, direct expenses, payments to outside vendors)

OVERHEAD COSTS:

A final charge is the cost of overhead, the additional costs in the training function not directly related to a particular program. The overhead category represents any training department cost not considered in the above calculations. Typical items include the cost of clerical support, the departmental office expenses, salaries of training managers, and other fixed costs. Some organizations obtain an estimate for allocation by dividing the total overhead by the number of program participant training days or hours for the year. This becomes a standard value to use in calculations. Typically this cost is $50 to $100 USD per participant.

1. General Overhead Allocation

TOTAL PROGRAM COSTS:

(this is the total of each detailed category)

There is no need to do the level of detail above for all costs. Sometimes a reasonable estimate of cost per person is fine. Just remember to think through the basic components of the seven costs we discussed. Where you have strategic, visible, or costly programs, the detailed analysis, using the templates above, can be helpful.

Human Capital ROI

Now let's discuss the first valuation model we introduced earlier, the human capital ROI. This operates on the premise that learning is in the business of improving human capital performance. What the human capital (people) do with improved performance is improve business results. Lastly, improved business results drive better shareholder value.

The goal is to calculate the positive change in human capital that has occurred because of the learning intervention. The major components of this valuation model are as follows:

- A Job Impact ROI. This is because the monetary value is linked to human capital, not to a specific business result so the evaluation is linked to Level 3, where impact is measured.

- Easy to use, practical, scalable, repeatable. The model's components exist on Post-Event, Follow-Up, and Manager evaluations, which can be distributed in mass and do not tax the respondent. Creating a standard for these evaluations makes it even easier to collect this information for every student, for every class.

- Provides a financial ROI relative to the improvement in human capital performance. We will use the baseline value of human capital, the salary, to multiply by the change in human capital performance. This is easily done and can be applied repeatedly throughout your learning interventions.

- Uses the Phillips ROI Principles of estimation, isolation, and adjustment. The valuation of human capital is based on these acceptable forms of measurement, adding credibility to your analysis.

- Part of a regular "balanced scorecard" for learning measurement. The value of the human capital ROI can be combined with other elements to produce a scorecard of metrics that tells the complete story of the program's value.

- Assumption is that human capital's value (i.e., salary) is like any other asset that has expected value and that can appreciate or depreciate over time. The use of salary as a monetary factor is not new. Earlier in the book we discussed the Nobel-Prize-winning work of Dr. Gary Becker who used wage rates. In addition, there was earlier work done by the Tennessee Valley Authority to calculate ROI on each class they held. They, too, used salary as the factor to value in financial terms, ROI.

Let's conduct a simple example of the Human Capital ROI model:

- Training cost per participant: $1000
- Average fully loaded salary of participant: $50,000
- **Estimate** performance improvement, including training: 30% (1)
- **Isolate** performance improvement due to training: 60% (of the 30% above) (2)
- **Isolate** performance relative to time spent performing those skills on the job: 20% (3)
- **Adjust** for bias, confidence, conservatism: 65% (4)
- Training impact on performance improvement, adjusted for bias: 30% x 60% x 20% x 65% = 2.34%
- Calculate monetized benefit = $50,000 x 2.34% = $1,170
- Calculate ROI = $1,170 - $1,000 = $170
- Calculate Benefit-to-Cost Ratio: $1,170 / $1,000 = $1.17

(1) Recalling the standard evaluations we discussed, ask a question directly on the survey for this estimate. This question is:

Given all factors, including this training, estimate how much your job performance related to the course subject matter will improve.
□0% □10% □20% □30% □40% □50% □60% □70% □80% □90% □100%

(2) Recalling the standard evaluations we
discussed, ask a question directly on the
survey for this isolation. This question is:

Based on your response to the prior question,
estimate how much of the improvement will be a
direct result of this training. (For example, if you feel
that half of your improvement is a direct result of the
training, enter 50% here.)
☐0% ☐10% ☐20% ☐30% ☐40% ☐50% ☐60% ☐70%
☐80% ☐90%☐100%

(3) Recalling the standard evaluations we
discussed, ask a question directly on the
survey for this isolation. This question is:

What percent of your total work time requires the
knowledge and skills presented in this training?
☐0% ☐10% ☐20% ☐30% ☐40% ☐50% ☐60% ☐70%
☐80% ☐90%☐100%

(4) The adjustment is based on research conducted by
KnowledgeAdvisors that indicates when, responding
to the aforementioned questions, respondents
overestimate by 35% or have a confidence average of
65%. Hence, we use 65% as the adjustment factor.

Let's look at a real-world example of the Human
Capital ROI model to see how it can work in practice.

An information technology training company had a
client who had made annual purchases of IT training

from the company. The client requested some form of value or benefit from the training they had purchased. This client was not able to provide significant resource access to gather the data and was looking for a roughly reasonable value to provide to their management to support the budget item for IT training in the future. They were looking to be good stewards of their budget and hence wanted to show an ROI.

The IT training company had been using the standard surveys we discussed, and for all training throughout the life cycle of the client relationship they had gathered this data on each participant evaluation. The IT training company also used an analytics tool that allowed them to filter their evaluation data by client after which they ran a query in the tool by this client. They then had the analytics tool calculate the human capital ROI, which they put into a standard template to be used for valuation communication with clients.

Figure 50 illustrates the Human Capital ROI for the client.

Figure 50. Human Capital ROI

Level 5 Return on Investment	Post Event
Costs(per person)	1,000
Monetary Benefits(per person)	3,500
Benefit to Cost Ratio	3.5
ROI Percentage	250%
Payback Period(months)	3.43

Source: KnowledgeAdvisors Metrics That Matter
Learning Analytics Technology

Another way the IT training company showed value
was through benchmarking. Because they used a
consistent standard for evaluation across all training
and all clients, they had a robust internal benchmark
database. Not only did they produce the financial
ROI the client requested, but they also gave
benchmark data. See Figure 51 for the results of this
analysis.

Figure 51: Benchmark Comparisons

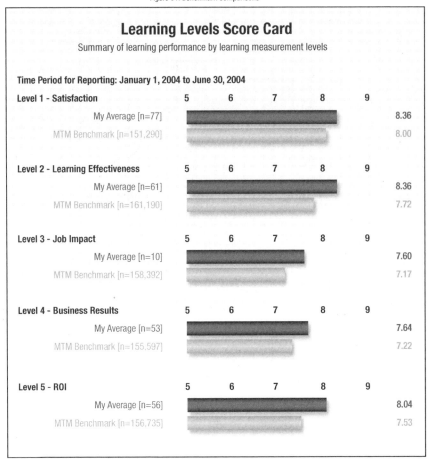

Source: KnowledgeAdvisors Metrics That Matter Learning Analytics Technology

In Figure 51, the blue bar represents the client data. The orange bar is all of the data from the IT provider for all of their clients. In this case, the client for whom this analysis is being conducted exceeds the benchmark, thereby indicating additional value. This report essentially maps each scored (Likert) question to a learning level and provides comparison data to give reasonable evidence of value via benchmark comparison.

The final effort made by the IT company was to get a quote from a senior manager who was credible and respected by the client. The company added this quote along with the aforementioned reports to tell the story of value in their final response to the client. The quote they received was the following:

"Prior to our relationship with [IT Training Company] we were not effectively providing a productivity baseline for our knowledge workers. Now we are definitely doing it."
— Manager, E-Learning/Technical Training, Iron Mountain

Use of a quote adds a layer of qualitative information and, if from a credible person, can paint a better picture.

Business Results ROI

If we know that our objective is to link learning to a specific set of business results, then a valuation model that does this is important. Instead of tying the financial value of learning to human capital based on salary, we will tie it to an indicator or the actual business result performance improvement.

Believe it or not, this model can also scale if you do not have time to gather actual results and do an up-front business needs assessment. The major components of the practical approach are as follows:

- A deeper Level 4 ROI. The approach goes after the business result(s), either estimated or actual, to derive value.

- Leverages technology to make it practical and scalable. Conditional drill-down questions on Internet- surveying technology can allow for respondents to answer more details on specific business results they felt had improved due to the program.

- Provides a financial ROI relative to the change in the business result(s) that prompted the training. If an actual business result can be measured for improvement with a financial value assigned, a financial ROI can be provided.

- Uses principles of estimation, isolation, and adjustment specific to the business result(s). Again, the Phillips ROI Process component is built into the model, making it credible.

- Part of a regular "balanced scorecard" for learning measurement. Again, metrics on business result(s) performance can be put on a scorecard of key indicators. We will discuss this in greater depth in the next chapter.

Let's walk through an example of how to calculate the value of learning relative to a specific business result whose performance was to have improved from learning.

- Training cost per participant: $5,000
- Business result significantly impacted: Sales
- Estimate/Calculate change in sales (pre- vs. post-training) = +20% (sales were $100,000 before training; now they are $120,000)(annualized)
- Isolate performance improvement due to training: 60% (of the 20% above)
- Adjust for bias, confidence, conservatism: 65%
- Training impact on sales adjusted for bias: Calculate monetized benefit = 20% x 60% x 65% = +7.8% (reported on the Business Result Scorecard); next steps can be done via the analyst worksheet
- Calculate monetized benefit = $100,000 x 7.8% = $7,800
- Calculate ROI = $7,800 - $5,000 = $2,800
- Calculate Benefit-to-Cost Ratio: $2,800 / $5,000 = $1.56

In an earlier discussion of templates, we mentioned a template to link learning to actual results both before and after the program. For strategic, visible, and costly programs, using a template like that is useful in determining the extent to which learning will impact the result both before and after the program.

However, let's look at an example of where that was not feasible. A customer education team of a technology company was charged with showing more value, in terms of results, to its customers. This team could not go into the customer and gather actual results. Even if they had been able to do that for one client, they could not have done that for all clients (numbering in the thousands). In addition, management wanted a single process to apply across customer education.

The team created a custom evaluation to deploy at the end of learning and sixty days later. They used conditional questions to ask a series of business results, followed by deeper questions, depending on the business result(s) selected earlier in the survey.

The question below was their lead-in question, designed to understand the results the participant felt were impacted.

> This training will have a significant impact on: (check all that apply)
> ☐ increasing quality ☐ increasing productivity
> ☐ increasing employee satisfaction
> ☐ decreasing costs ☐ increasing sales
> ☐ increasing customer satisfaction
> ☐ decreasing cycle time

The next questions address the issues that would arise had the participant checked "increasing productivity" in answer to the prior question:

BUSINESS RESULTS-PRODUCTIVITY
If you selected "Increasing productivity" as a
business result, please answer the following
questions:

Given all factors, including this training,
estimate how much productivity will increase:
☐0% ☐5% ☐10% ☐15% ☐20% ☐25% ☐30%
☐35% ☐40% ☐45% ☐50% ☐55% ☐60% ☐65%
☐70% ☐75% ☐80% ☐85% ☐90% ☐95% ☐100%

Based on your response to the prior question,
estimate how much of the improvement will be
a direct result of this training (for example, if
you believe that half of your improvement is a
direct result of the training, enter 50%):
☐0% ☐5% ☐10% ☐15% ☐20% ☐25% ☐30%
☐35% ☐40% ☐45% ☐50% ☐55% ☐60% ☐65%
☐70% ☐75% ☐80% ☐85% ☐90% ☐95%☐100%

The end result is that this organization collected
thousands of data points in a few months and had an
interesting story to tell.

Some highlights of their data collection efforts are as
follows:

- 20% improvement in user productivity after
  completing training class

- 24% improvement in cycle time

- 22% improvement in quality

- >90% felt that the training was a worthwhile investment for their employees

In addition, they received great quotes from their customers to supplement the data. For example, this quote appeared in a press release they issued to share results with their customer base: "We see great value in being able to link our education courses to an increase in productivity."

Figure 52 has an example of a scorecard that analyzed the results of their efforts.

Figure 52: Business Results Scorecard

Business Results Scorecard

Business Results: Productivity (analyze and monetize this result)	Post Event
Total percent improvement in productivity, including training.............................	51%
Training's contribution to improved productivity	57%
Percent improvement due to training	29.1%
Adjustment factor for confidence in estimations	65%
Adjusted percent improvement due to training	18.9%

Business Results: Quality (analyze and monetize this result)	Post Event
Total percent improvement in quality, including training.................................	54%
Training's contribution to improved quality..	57%
Percent improvement due to training	30.8%
Adjustment factor for confidence in estimations	65%
Adjusted percent improvement due to training	20%

Business Results: Increasing Customer Satisfaction (analyze and monetize this result)	Post Event
Total percent improvement in customer satisfaction, including training	52%
Training's contribution to improved customer satisfaction	57%
Percent improvement due to training	29.6%
Adjustment factor for confidence in estimations	65%
Adjusted percent improvement due to training	19.3%

Source: KnowledgeAdvisors Metrics That Matter Learning Analytics Technology

Figure 52 shows how the principles of estimation/isolation/adjustment worked to yield the conservative business result percentage changes.

Had a specific client requested a more detailed analysis, the learning team could have deployed an approach in which the actual result and "measure/isolate/adjust" could be used instead.

Although articulated earlier in the book, Figure 53 shows the Analyst Worksheet used by the L&D group when the client wanted to see the actual results isolated and adjusted. This was a rare request because (a) the data here was reasonable and not time-consuming to gather, (b) the customer had little time to do more than this, and (c) the actual data was subjective and not worth pursuing as it had little additional credibility over the data that had already been collected.

Nonetheless, the ability to "measure/isolation/adjust" using the actual business result is a great way to yield more precise measures.

Figure 53: Analyst Worksheet

1) Name your worksheet: | Sales Training

2) Name the business result (ex. Increased quality, annualized) | Increased Sales, annualized

3) Define your business result performance measure (ex. Defects per unit, annualized) | Sales Revenue per year

4) Estimate the quantitative metric for each performance measure:

Important note: all items in this section must be annualized (ex. 1 month of data is 100 unit sales representing $1000, input 1200 unit sales representing $12,000 as an annualized number).

	Group Trained Metric	Monetary Value	Control Group Metric (Optional)	Monetary Value
Estimate the metric as measured **BEFORE** the training:	100	10000	100	10000
Estimate the metric as measured **AFTER** the training:	150	15000	110	11000
Total change in metric:	50%	5000	10%	1000

5) Isolate root causes of the total percentage change in metric.

Please input the percentage of the change in the metric that was driven by these causes (total should equal 100%)

	Group Trained Metric	Monetary Value	Control Group Metric (Optional)	Monetary Value
Personnel:	0	0	0	0
Technology:	20	1000	20	200
External factors:	0	0	0	0
Procedure/Policy:	30	1500	50	500
Incentives:	0	0	0	0
Training:	50	2500	0	0
Other:	0	0	30	300
Total (should equal 100%)	100%	5000	100%	1000

6) Adjustment factor for confidence in estimations: (percentage) | 65

Source: Metrics That Matter Learning Analytics Technology by KnowledgeAdvisors

The tool in Figure 53 enabled the learning team to conduct a more comprehensive business impact and ROI analysis. The tool also allowed them to store actual business results tied to multiple programs and to show training impact and ROI. It follows the 'measure/isolate/adjust' model. Here we use the actual result measure as opposed to an estimated figure.

Impact Study

The final model is the Impact Study model. An impact study is a deeper analysis that is done a smaller percentage of the time (about 5 to 10%) due to the resource requirements.

It is best to apply this model after undergoing ROI certification through the ROI Institute because the Institute offers a five-day workshop on how to comprehensively measure learning programs, after which a certification is issued.

The key elements of an impact study are as follows:

- Participants can be certified to do it
- Formal step-by-step process
- Defined cost components
- More comprehensive data collection instruments for end-of-program and post-program follow-up analysis
- Detailed cost wizard for input of comprehensive costs per study

- Detailed action-plan templates for input of comprehensive business results and impact data per participant
- Business results analysis for each participant's business results

Impact studies leverage more comprehensive isolation techniques, such as control group analysis, trend line analysis and statistical analysis, as opposed to expert or participant estimation. They are therefore more resource-intensive and are suggested when a specific learning program meets one or more of the following criteria:

1. Visible
2. Costly
3. Strategic

Some examples of impact study results are as follows:

Sales Training Program: Trained employees' average retail weekly sales were $12,075 vs. $10,449 for similar employees who were not trained.

Performance Management Program: A performance management program at a restaurant generated over $170,000 in benefits directly tied to the training, yet the training cost less than $50,000.

Master's Degree Program for Federal Agency: Goal was to reduce high turnover. One year after the program, turnover was 34% for employees NOT in the program and 3% for employees IN the program. The program yielded a benefit-to-cost ratio of over 2 to 1.

Following is an illustration of a write-up derived from an impact study done for a leadership program at a major cable company. In this case, the cable company used evaluations as a component of estimation and isolation. This summary is a nice example of the Human Capital model taken to the next level to be written up more formally as an impact study.

Appendix. Leadership Program Impact Study

Executive Summary
In response to a request from one of the directors in Cable Company A's Raleigh Division, a leadership development workshop was conducted in September 2005 for the nine directors who accepted the invitation to attend. The directors who attended were from sales, marketing, collections, commercial services, finance, network operations, and construction. The program delivered was Franklin Covey's Four Roles of Leadership. It was a two-day workshop with a week between the two sessions. Pre-work included choosing a real project or initiative to work on during and after the workshop. Individual coaching was offered to all participants, and four accepted.

An ROI impact study was conducted for this program because of its high-level content, visibility, and participants. Using the ROI Methodology developed by Dr. Jack Phillips, we developed objectives, gathered data, and evaluated results in five levels of learning: reaction / satisfaction / planned action, learning, application, business impact, and return on investment. Taking a conservative approach to costs and benefits, we calculated an ROI of 825% based upon participants' estimates of their productivity increase and the amount of that increase that was due to the training.

It appears that the Four Roles of Leadership program, at least under certain conditions, is effective. It is recommended that the program be expanded to other groups of managers within the division and to directors in other divisions. It should also be considered for inclusion in the regionalization plan for leadership development.

Background
Cable Company A's Raleigh Division is based in Morrisville, North Carolina, and employs approximately 1,700 people. The service area covers most of central North Carolina and has over 500,000 subscribers to digital video, high-speed data, and voice-over Internet protocol (VOIP) digital phone service. In the organization chart, there are four levels of management reporting to the division president. They are: vice presidents, directors, managers, and supervisors.

In June of 2005, one of the directors submitted a request for some leadership training to the division manager of Training and Development. After some discussion of objectives, it was determined that it would be provided in-house. The program selected was Franklin Covey's Four Roles of Leadership. Participation was to be voluntary for the directors and was scheduled for September 7 and 14.

Very little, if any, management or leadership training had been provided for the management in the division and most directors were very excited about attending the training. Nine directors registered for the two-day workshop. The training would take place at a nearby hotel to minimize distractions and to get away from the day-to-day operations of the directors' respective departments.

Objectives

The Four Roles of Leadership workshop helps managers identify and develop four critical abilities of true leaders: *pathfinding, aligning, empowering,* and *modeling.* It is designed to improve the results of the participants by affording an opportunity to apply these four roles.

Pathfinding is creating a blueprint for success and has these objectives:
- Understand stakeholder needs (global trends, customer requirements)
- Develop and articulate vision and purpose
- Sharpen strategic focus on key priorities

Aligning is creating a technically elegant system of work and has these objectives:
- Translate key priorities into practical action
- Align systems and processes to achieve key priorities
- Focus on organization outcomes

Empowering is releasing talent, energy, and contribution of people and has these objectives:

- Foster commitment to key priorities
- Celebrate and leverage diversity
- Build effective teams
- Manage performance in a win-win mode

And finally, *modeling* is building trust with others by walking your talk and has these objectives:
- Build relationships of trust
- Model ethical behavior and personal integrity
- Provide rich, productive input and feedback

One of the key components of the program is the pre-work. Prior to attending, the participants select a real-world initiative or project. They bring this initiative to the workshop and work on it approximately 20% of class time as they learn each role. The planning they accomplish in class is designed to help them achieve their objectives after the event.

In light of today's business climate of increased accountability and budget scrutiny, this program was selected for an ROI impact study because of the high level of the participants in the organization and because of the importance placed upon the initiatives to be worked on during and after the program. In addition to objectives of the program, the following objectives for participants were identified for each of the learning levels that were measured:

- Begin work on their initiative (Level 1)

- Have a positive reaction to the content and materials, and to their anticipated application (Level 1)
- Have a positive reaction to the facilitator (Level 1)
- Increase their knowledge and skill in leadership (Level 2)
- Focus application of at least one of the four roles (Level 3)
- Increase productivity (Level 4)
- Yield a Return on investment (ROI) of at least 50% (Level 5)

Methodology
The Phillips ROI Methodology was used for this impact study. This measurement and evaluation process, which was built on the earlier work of Donald Kirkpatrick's four levels of learning effectiveness, collects measures on six levels:
- Reaction, satisfaction, and planned action
- Learning
- Application and implementation
- Business impact
- Return on investment
- Intangible measures

Evaluation planning was the first step and was vitally important. It was during the planning phase that we defined our purpose, determined the appropriate levels of evaluation, and developed our objectives. Our primary purpose was to determine whether the program accomplished its objectives in a cost-effective manner. To realize that purpose required calculating ROI and developing appropriate objectives for all levels up to and including ROI.

The next step was *data collection*. We used the questionnaires that are built into our learning analytics system, Metrics That Matter (MTM), to gather, store, and analyze the data. Immediately after the event, a Web-based questionnaire was sent to the attendees. It asked them to rate their experience in seven areas: instructor, environment, courseware, learning effectiveness, job impact, business results, and return on investment. The participants were asked to rate the statements by using a seven-point Likert scale or choosing a percentage. There were three questions in which participants could enter comments, and a yes/no question about whether they would like to be contacted about advanced or complementary courses. This data gave us the Levels 1 (reaction, satisfaction, and planned action) and 2 (learning measures).

Sixty days after the workshop, a follow-up questionnaire was sent via e-mail to the participants. This tool gathered information that measures Level 3 (application, implementation) and Level 4 (business impact). The categories in the questionnaire are learning effectiveness, job impact, business results, support tools, return on investment, and feedback on how we can make the training more relevant. In the category of learning effectiveness, we wanted to know whether the participants learned anything new. Regarding job impact, we were interested in how much they have been able to apply what they learned.

In the business results section, the participants estimated whether their performance has improved, how much it has improved, and how much of the improvement was a direct result of the training received. In support tools, we wanted to know whether the learning is supported on the job. In the return-on-investment questions, we were asking qualitatively whether they think the training was a worthwhile investment.

MTM is essentially a data warehouse or data mart that allows the information to be reported on in a way that makes decision making easier. Benchmarks can be set internally or against other organizations in MTM's database. Alarms can be set to send alerts when a specific measure falls below a certain score. This allows real-time proactive response by management instead of reacting after the fact when it is too late to do anything about it. There is also predictive capability in the dynamic reporting engine. All calculations are automated in the system, which saves administrative time and allows more time for analysis, decision making, and predictions. Instead of offering activity-based information, MTM shows effectiveness and impact.

Costs

To calculate ROI, we needed to determine the program's costs. The costs are fully loaded and include the participants' time, facilitator's time, materials, facilities, evaluation time, administration, and coaching. They are shown below:

Participants' time

(9 X 20 hrs. X $65/hr)	$11,750
Facilitator's time	
(1 X 30 hrs. X $50/hr)	$1,500
Facilities/meals	
(2 days X $350/day)	$700
Administrative time	
(4 hrs. X $25/hr)	$100
Coaching	
(16 hrs. of coach and participant time)	$1,800
Materials	
(9 X $100)	$900
Evaluation time	
(6 hrs. X $50/hr)	$300
Total	$17,050
Cost per participant	$1,900

All salaries are based upon average (if not known) or actual figures (if known) plus 35% for benefits and overhead.

Taking this conservative approach, all costs, direct and nondirect, are included in the ROI calculations. Besides being conservative, it helps identify training costs that may have been hidden before and gives a more accurate picture of the financial impact of training. For costs, when in doubt we include it. For benefits, when in doubt we leave it out.

Results
Measures were taken on all five levels of impact. Care was taken to ensure that we were as conservative in our analysis as we could be. Where there was doubt, costs were overstated and benefits were understated. The results for each level plus some intangible benefits are shown below.

Reaction and Satisfaction (Level 1)

This section shows the data collected from the participants immediately after the event to measure their reactions to the program and levels of satisfaction with various parts of the process. The categories measured were: instructor, environment, courseware, potential job impact, potential business results, and anticipated return on investment. The vehicle used to gather and store the data was MTM's Post-Event Survey that is sent via e-mail with a link to the survey. The reports generated were the Class Summary and the Learning Levels Scorecard. The scores shown are the average of the participants for each part and are based upon a seven-point Likert scale. Eight of the nine participants responded to the survey.

Instructor	6.52
Environment	6.00
Courseware	6.47
Job Impact	6.50
Business Results	6.38
Return on Investment	6.56
Total	**6.45**

These scores fall well above our target of 6.00 and show a high degree of satisfaction at this level.

Learning (Level 2)

There was no specific assessment or test for this program; however, the participants were asked to respond to two items on the Post-Event Survey. First, they rated (on the Likert scale) their response to the statement "I learned new knowledge and skills from this training." Next, they were asked to rate their increase in skill level or knowledge of the content before versus after the training. The scale was from 0% to 100% in increments of 10%.

Learning Effectiveness	6.13
Percent Increase	35%

Our goals for these were 5.75 and 20%, respectively.

Application and Implementation (Level 3)
This section shows the success in implementing and applying the new skills and knowledge. The data is received through MTM's Follow-up Survey, which is sent out via e-mail with a link to the survey. It measures job impact in five areas estimated by the participants. The five areas are:
- Application of knowledge/skills to the job (Likert scale)
- Amount of work time requiring the knowledge/skills (%)
- Criticality of training to the job (%)
- Amount of training actually applied to the job (%)
- Post-training support (Likert scale)

The overall averages are shown in the table below:

Application of knowledge/skills to the job	6.00 (Likert scale)
Amount of work time requiring the knowledge/skills	72%

Criticality of training to the job	74%
Amount of training actually applied to job	57%
Post-training Support	4.83 (Likert scale)

Our goal for the application of knowledge and skills was 5.50. There were no goals for the three percentage estimates. The goal for post-training support was 5.50. The scores show a solid application of the training despite below-target support scores. Further analysis of the support section shows the scores on the individual items that make up this section.

Participant materials useful on the job	5.86 (Likert scale)
Set expectations with manager prior to training	2.40 (Likert scale)
Determined use of training after the training	4.33 (Likert scale)
Provided adequate resources to apply training on the job	6.40 (Likert scale)

The lowest scores, setting expectations with the manager prior to training and determining the use of training after the training, could have been improved by suggesting this to the participants. Discussions with the manager can help increase learning and application. They are also an excellent way to confirm that expectations are clear and agreed upon.

Business Impact (Level 4)

The business impact measure that drove this level of evaluation was increasing productivity. The data was gathered by participants' estimates on the MTM Follow-up Survey. This section estimates the job performance change, measured in productivity, and the amount of change that is due to the program. It is summarized below.

Training's estimated impact on improved productivity	5.57 (Likert scale)
Total percent improvement in productivity	38.00
Training's contribution to improved performance	77.00
Percent of work time requiring the knowledge and skills	72.00
Percent improvement due to training (0.38 X 0.77 X 0.72 X 100; from rows 2-4)	21.07
Adjustment factor for confidence in estimation	65.00%
Adjusted percent improvement due to training	13.70%

The average percent improvement in productivity was 38.00%. But many factors could have contributed to this improvement. We needed to isolate the effect that training had on the productivity increase. For this study, the participants' estimates method was used. They were asked to estimate the amount of the productivity increase that was due to the training. The average estimate was 77.00%. To further refine the estimate, we asked the participants how much of their work time requires the knowledge and skills acquired during the training. The average response was 72.00%. If we multiply 38% (.38) by 77% (.77) by 72% (.72), the product is .2107 or 21.07%. Because these estimates are not completely accurate, to be conservative we adjust it once more for a confidence factor in the participants' estimates. We used a confidence factor of 65% (.65) because some research has shown that people tend to overestimate by 35%. By multiplying .2107 by .65 X 100, we arrive at a net improvement due to training of 13.70%. This increase is consistent with the 35% increase in learning (Level 2) estimate and the 57% application estimate. By showing earlier that we had an increase in knowledge and skills and that they were applied on the job, we can at least make a claim that the program had an impact on the productivity increase based upon the participants' estimates.

Conversely, if there had not been an increase in Level 2 or Level 3, it would have been difficult to claim that training had any effect at all. This is called the chain of impact and is vital in being able to isolate the effects of training. It is possible, however, to have an improvement in Levels 2 and/or 3 but no improvement in Level 4. Even though learning and application took place, there could have been obstacles between learning and application, or application and business impact that hindered further improvement. Having this chain of impact gives the analyst or performance consultant a starting point to troubleshoot for the cause of the breakdown.

The follow-up survey also asks participants to record specific business results that were significantly impacted by the training. The percentages in the table below are the percentages of participants responding that the specific business result was significantly impacted.

Increasing quality	85.71%
Decreasing costs	14.29%
Increasing productivity	71.43%
Increasing sales	14.29%
Increasing customer satisfaction	42.86%
Increasing employee satisfaction	85.71%

ROI (Level 5)
For our purposes, we defined return on investment (ROI) as a measure of net program benefits to program costs. Mathematically, it looks like this:

ROI (%) = Net Program Benefits X 100
Program Costs
Net Benefits are the program benefits minus the program costs. Program costs are all of the fully loaded costs (direct and indirect) of the program.
Before we could calculate, we needed to convert the business impact measure, productivity, to a monetary

value. We did this using the Human Capital ROI Method. With this method, an assumption is made that the monetary value of a participant is equivalent to his or her fully loaded compensation (salary plus benefits plus overhead). The program benefits are obtained by multiplying the adjusted percent improvement due to training (13.70% or .137) by the fully loaded compensation average director salary plus a 35% adjustment for benefits and overhead).

Program Benefits per person =

.137 X $128,250 = $17,570.25

Program Costs per person = $1900

ROI = $17,570.25 X 100

$1900

ROI = 824.75%

Payback period 1.3 months

Intangible Measures

Not all benefits of a training program can be converted into monetary value; nonetheless, they are still considered to be positive results. These are called intangible measures and some were mentioned in the follow-up survey in the participants' comments. The intangible benefits noted by our participants were improvements in:

- Teamwork
- Communication between departments
- Planning
- Delegating
- Self-awareness and observation
- Stress reduction

Although we could not place a dollar figure on these improvements, most would agree that they contribute to organizational success.

Barriers and Enablers

There were few barriers to the success of the project. The primary one, which seems ubiquitous, is the general busy-ness of the participants. During the workshop, several discussions among the participants centered around the perceived shifting priorities of their bosses, causing the participants to jump from project to project without being able to complete anything to their satisfaction. This was an area of frustration for them. But there are enablers that are directly linked to this barrier.

During the workshop, we discussed the importance of planning and prioritizing, and we suggested techniques for being more effective in this area. The four participants who chose to continue with post-event coaching are focusing their coaching program on values-based time management.

Another enabling factor that should not be ignored is the participants' hunger for training. As directors, most of them had some kind of management/leadership training in their careers but not much lately. As a result, they were highly motivated before, during, and after the workshop. Anecdotal feedback also indicated that they benefited from communicating with the directors from other departments and expressed a desire to have regular sessions together.

The learning atmosphere was enhanced by conducting the workshop off-site. Most of the participants agreed that if the workshop had been in one of the training rooms in the Division office, there would have been many more distractions and interruptions. Only once did a cell phone interrupt the class, although some participants were sneaking peeks at their Blackberries from time to time.

Conclusions and Recommendations

It appears that the Four Roles of Leadership training program, under the right circumstances, is an effective program. It produced a very high ROI (825%). Even if it is off by a factor of ten, it is a high ROI (82.5%). Training programs with such a high ROI should be expanded to other management groups within the Raleigh Division or to directors in other divisions, or both. A pilot program could be implemented for each of the groups, followed by a similar ROI impact study. It is also recommended that the program be considered for the Cable Company A Carolinas Region's regionalization initiative for training. Under this initiative, there will be standardization of content for most training, based upon best practices at all five divisions in the region. This initiative is just getting started and an impact study such as this could provide enough evidence of the program's effectiveness to be included as a part of a regional leadership development program.

Although it was not done for this study, the differences in survey scores for the participants who engaged in follow-up coaching and those who did not could be analyzed for statistical significance using the analysis of variance (ANOVA) technique for comparing the mean scores of the two groups. This would tell us if coaching adds any value to the program. This could be done as soon as there is a large enough sample size to make it meaningful.

As part of training governance, an advisory council should define targets for the percentage of programs evaluated at each of the five levels of the ROI Methodology. This advisory council should be comprised of members of senior management, the learning and development staff, and members of the three primary customers of training: Customer Operations, Technical Operations, and Sales & Marketing. These targets should balance the value of the evaluations and the time it takes to do them, and should take into consideration such factors as visibility, cost, potential impact, strategic importance, and politics.

IX. Key Performance Indicators and Dashboards

Key performance indicators can be produced onto scorecards or dashboards so that a senior leader of learning or those outside learning can understand the health of the learning organization.

Let's start by defining what a dashboard is. A dashboard is a convenient place for vital information organized into a graphical representation that is both easy to use and easy to understand.

There are five steps you'll want to follow when designing a dashboard for L&D. These are as follows:

1. Research learning metrics.
2. Identify macro learning constructs.
3. Build micro learning indicators.
4. Build a process to collect and report.
5. Design technology and templates for support.

The first step is to research what is already being done in this area. This gives you creative insight to draw upon for your own dashboards.

There has been some excellent research from the Learning & Development Roundtable on this topic. The Learning and Development Roundtable (LDR) is the world's premier network of learning executives.

The central focus of their work is helping learning executives to direct their investments toward the greatest opportunities to create value for their organizations through precise alignment of learning solutions, infrastructures, and processes with the strategic priorities of the business.

The LDR profiled several organizations and the dashboards they use.

Other sources of insight for dashboards and scorecards in the learning and development space include the following:

• American Society of Training & Development (ASTD). The ASTD offers a wealth of resources for measurement and evaluation, including an evaluation and ROI community that could be particularly helpful.

• ROI Institute. The ROI Institute, Inc. — a research, benchmarking, and consulting organization — provides workshops, publications, and consulting services on the ROI Methodology. Through their Web site, they distribute information and support the ROI efforts of professionals and organizations around the world.

• KnowledgeAdvisors. A technology and solutions company, KnowledgeAdvisors specializing in helping L&D organizations measure, communicate, and improve the effectiveness of learning investments.

The next step is to identify macro learning constructs. These are a small, well-balanced set of broad learning metric classifications that summarize the results of the entire L&D organization. Constructs are a mile wide and an inch deep.

The key macro learning constructs that can yield an ideal dashboard or scorecard include the following:

Operational - Activity constructs (how much we train)
Performance - Optimization constructs (how well we train)
Financial - Budget/Fiscal constructs (how much it costs)
Cultural - Supportive environment constructs (how conducive it is to learning)

Operational constructs address the question of how much we train. These are volume-based metrics that one can typically get from a learning management or registration system. They include items such as number of classes held or number of students trained. It is important to understand these metrics to ensure that the L&D organization continues to have adequate throughput.

Performance constructs address the question of how well we train. It attempts to look at what is done with the existing budget. It can examine anything from satisfaction to business result linkage.

Financial constructs address the question of how much it costs and what monetary benefit was derived. It also looks at whether or not the learning linked to the bottom-line financial impact.

Cultural constructs address the question of how supportive the organizational culture is to viewing learning as strategic. So it answers the question "How conducive is learning to the environment?", especially in times of tumultuous change such as merger, acquisition, divestiture, or change in senior management.

These four quadrants create a small, well-balanced family of metrics that can give a senior executive enough information about the L&D group without breaking into the details.

The next step is to identify the micro learning indicators. These are a set of quantifiable performance measures linked to the macro learning construct that are tracked over time. These micro indicators are a mile deep and an inch wide.

For the operational metrics, some examples of micro indicators that might fall under this macro construct include the following:

- # of students trained
- instructor utilization rate
- e-learning utilization rate
- average class size
- speed to market (speed to need)

- staff to management ratio
- delivery mix
- survey response rates
- class completion or cancellation rates

For the performance metrics, some examples of micro indicators that might fall under this macro construct include the following:

- Level 1 satisfaction scores
- instructor performance
- courseware quality
- learning effectiveness (test scores)
- time to job impact

Business Results Linkage such as Sales, Quality, Cycle Time, Productivity, Customer Satisfaction, Cost Savings etc.

Regarding the business results, there are two approaches:

1. Business results may be estimated and isolated to training, and adjusted for confidence. Thus, L&D can track how they have linked to such results. This can help L&D articulate their share of the performance change.

2. Business results may be simply tracked regardless of how L&D impacted it. This can help L&D to: (a) track actual results to understand if they are trending in the right direction, (b) keep their finger on the pulse of

what is important to the organization, (c) react quickly when the metric goes in the wrong direction and (d) have a seat at the table

For the financial metrics, some examples of micro indicators that might fall under this macro construct include the following:

- cost per student day
- L&D cost as a % of payroll
- L&D budget to actual
- L&D investment mix
- revenue growth
- Human Capital Contribution Margin (L&D expense and payroll divided into sales)
- profit margin
- L&D ROI
- productivity per employee

With financial metrics, you'll see traditional metrics like cost per student day or L&D cost as a percent of payroll. However, some of the more important metrics are revenue growth, profit margin, and human capital contribution margin.

One of the most important of all of these is productivity per employee. If learning is in the business of improving human capital performance, then this measure, which is a financial metric for productivity of human capital, becomes essential.

In fact, Charles Knight, Chairman Emeritus of Emerson Electric, once spoke to a group of Chicago-based learning professionals. He illustrated the need for L&D managers to measure productivity. He began his presentation by showing EBITDA trends, stock price, and revenue growth trends. Soon enough an L&D professional in the audience posed the question, "What does this have to do with learning?" Mr. Knight responded with two statements. The first was that the Emerson corporate university had been named after him so that he had indeed supported learning in his twenty-seven years of uninterrupted growth.

However, it was his second statement that crystallized the need for L&D executives to measure productivity. He showed some charts that resembled Figure 54 below.

Figure 54: Productivity

OR

Source: : Charles Knight presentation, Chicagoland Learning Leaders Conference, October 10, 2006

Although Figure 54 is basic, it is very important to a CEO, COO, CFO, or any other 'C'-level person. C-level people are successful if they grow revenue while keeping the employee base constant. This means they are utilizing existing resources with optimal productivity to do this.

Alternatively, the bottom box shows that in a period of stagnant revenues, CEOs want to achieve that while decreasing the total number of employees.

These figures are important to CEOs for many reasons. First, the top box helps CEOs get their bonuses. The bottom box helps them keep their jobs.

The other reason these are important is that they are based on financial statement figures that a CEO can easily understand. Revenue comes right from the income statement. Number of employees is in the notes to the financial statement. So these are objective and fact-based.

The final and most important reason an L&D manager should use this measure is that it is the ultimate human capital performance indicator. If this measure is increasing over lengthy periods of time, then it is a pretty good sign that the organization is getting more and more out of its human capital. This means L&D is doing their job by increasing human capital performance.

For the cultural metrics, some examples of micro indicators that might fall under this macro construct include the following:

- training eligibility
- average hrs of training per employee
- available tuition reimbursement
- management support
- internal validation
- external validation

Traditional measures are eligibility, training hours per employee, and tuition reimbursement.

Nontraditional measures include management support.
This is a measure that can be easily obtained by asking the right questions on surveys to understand the culture and its conduciveness to learning. Here are some responses to questions designed to monitor management support:

"My manager and I set expectations for this training."
"After training, my manager and I discussed how I will use the training on the job."
"I was provided adequate resources (time, money, equipment) to successfully apply this training on my job."

Track the replies to questions about management support on follow-up surveys and you will understand the direction of management support.

The other cultural indicators include internal and external validation.

Internal validation is achieved after creating cases internally to serve as examples that a key program or initiative was successful and value-added. These cases are concise yet articulate summaries of qualitative and quantitative information that anyone can read to understand the context of the program and its value.

Internal validation is important because, as the organizational culture changes with mergers, acquisitions, divestitures, and changes in management, L&D needs to insulate itself as best as it can.

Below is an example of a case done for a not-for-profit that had a popular executive book club program under scrutiny by the board. The case articulates the qualitative and quantitative benefits.

The Book Club Is a Powerful Tool for Executives to Improve Skills and Drive Results

Background
It began as an idea and has blossomed into one of the most value-added tools we offer executives. The Book Club provides opportunities to learn and apply creative insights from the world's foremost business thinkers. The Club provides rigor in accomplishing the reading and distillation of critical concepts that

would likely otherwise never occur in the busy lives of the executives. Last but certainly not least, the executives absolutely value the opportunity to discuss the concepts of these books with their peers who have the same challenges they do. In the words of Jane M, "The highlight is feedback from others in like organizations with like challenges."

Cost and Time Savings for Leaders
Business book clubs, with appropriate book selection and experienced facilitation, can be low-cost, time-effective ways for busy executives to grow professionally.

One executive has been given permission to receive CEU credits for book club participation. Such an opportunity saves executives considerable costs associated with attending workshops or other programs. This is important when they have limited funds for professional development.

Several leaders of the Book Club reported that the structure of the Club helps them save considerable time in their learning and development. They can read on their own time and don't have to be away from the operations they manage to gain high-quality leadership development.

The quality of the programs is seen in a recent evaluation exercise whereby 80% of Book Club participants rated it with the highest satisfaction and 98% with the top three highest marks. Further, an excellent indicator of value is the fact that 80% of participants would recommend it to others.

Intangible Benefits of the Book Club
Although there are real benefits from the Book Club that will be discussed, there are numerous intangible benefits that accrue from participating in a program like this.

First, the Book Club allows for peer-level exploration and discussion. This form of structured networking was a key benefit cited by participants.

Second, the take-aways from the Book Club are turning executives into better leaders. By focusing on concepts such as change management, service excellence, and innovation, there is a renewed optimism among participants that they can make a positive difference in their organizations. Per Noel J., CFO, "Am I a better manager, leader, and strategic thinker? I certainly think so."

Further, the concepts and materials from the Book Club are disseminated throughout the organizations. This is seen in the data. For example, 74% of program attendees have taken ideas from the Book Club and implemented them on the job. In addition, 90% of attendees share the books with other members of their organizations. This trickle-down impact is a significant intangible not to be overlooked.

To Fred S., Vice President of Operations, "The results should be a stronger, more interactive environment where we will have a much more educated level of leadership who will be able to bring a balanced understanding of all the dynamics impacting our program to our leadership teams."

Several executives described the tangible benefits of the Book Club. The next section discusses these.

Tangible Benefits from the Book Club
The Book Club has had profound effects on the individual and organizational results of its participants. Results ranging from increased contract revenue to better time management have accrued, due in part to the Book Club.

Sal G., Director of Clinical Services, cited multiple results from his Book Club experience. For example, after reading *Organized for Success*, Sal was able to better manage paperwork. After reading *Manager of Choice*, Sal was able to recruit and retain employees with greater success. Finally, after discussing the book *Becoming a Strategic Leader*, Sal created a new product line of autism services.

Jane M. has been a participant in the Book Club for a few years. After reading *Organized for Success*, Jane posted major concepts from the book in her office to keep her on task. She has saved up to an hour a day by simply applying the concepts of the book to make her more productive.

Jane also utilized concepts of the Book Club to solve a major problem: employee turnover. Prior to implementing ideas gleaned from Book Club, turnover was 125%. After implementing the ideas, turnover declined to 88% — due in part to the success of the Book Club.

In terms of financial benefits, the Book Club has also made a tangible impact. As a result of taking action following discussions surrounding the book *Governance as Leadership*, Wayne M., President/CEO, applied for and won a $323,000 grant. Per Wayne, "The Book Club best practices have bled over into the operations and we're seeing results because of it."

A major goal of the organization is to help executives obtain increased contract revenue. In the case of Mark W., this is precisely what happened as a result of his participation in the Book Club. Mark has a longstanding customer whose average annual contract revenues increased by 50% (from $250,000 per year to $500,000) when Mark applied some of the concepts from the books discussed in the Book Club, specifically *From Good to Great*. Mark stated that the book and the ensuing discussions encouraged him to take a chance and think in a service-oriented and innovative way to expand services with this customer.

Concluding Thoughts
Although the Book Club can be expensive to administer, costs can be controlled through such efforts as collaborating with the facilitator to reduce facilitation fees or institute direct facilitation, conducting fewer cycles, or offering repeat sessions.

The question, however, should not be about removing the program from the curricula. The quantitative data clearly shows that the curricula are of high quality resulting in high job impact. The interviews and testimonials gathered validated the quantitative data by identifying numerous intangible and tangible benefits that executives found from the participation in the Book Club.

Interestingly, over 50% of the Book Club participants cite the club as their ONLY form of training. These are critical executives, and they articulate a desire to continue to partake in the Book Club.

Ultimately, the Book Club adds value. It fulfills the mission of the organization to help executives be in a better position to meet the requirements of government contracts and ultimately win the work. At the end of the day, that is the main objective of the organization. Continued efforts to provide flexible and innovative programs like the Book Club send a strong signal to executives that the organization is committed to supporting them and is a valued partner in helping them be successful. This is a positive message that should continue to be delivered.

A final form of cultural metrics is external validation. External validation occurs when the L&D organization goes outside its own organization and participates in specific L&D actions to showcase its thought leadership among peers. Sometimes, sadly enough, this external validation reinforces the need of the internal organization to value L&D. Examples of external validation include the following:

- Article profiling the L&D organization or its leader
- L&D organization applying for and winning awards
- L&D organization speaking at conferences or events

After you've thought through the macro and micro indicators for your L&D dashboard, you should begin to think about the process you will follow to collect, store, process, and report the data.

As with any other data, it is important to leverage technology, standards, and templates. Also, this data might best be gathered on a quarterly basis at the dashboard.

Figure 55 below shows an example of some dashboard templates that could be created to store and track the indicators in the prior section.

Figure 55: Dashboard Templates

Search	Edit	Help

USD—United States Dollars ▼ Go

Enter Business Result Data

ABC L&D Operational Dashboard Metrics

Tracking Form Name:	ABC L&D Operational Dashboard Metrics
Start Date for Data Input:	Jan. 1, 2006
Frequency:	Monthly
Period Ending:	Jan. 31, 2006

Custom Business Results	Data Type	Desired Trend	Goal	Actual
No. of Students Trained	Integer	Increasing	100	50
E-Learning Utilization Rate	Percent	Increasing	75.00%	25.00%
Speed to Market (Days to Respond to Client Training Need)	Integer	Decreasing	15	45
Instructor Utilization Rate (Days of Instructor Time)	Integer	Increasing	85	85

Download History	Run Report

Save	Save and Move On

Figure 55 shows the input template. The basic items you would want to have on the dashboard input template are as follows:

- date range
- metric
- data type (percentage, integer, currency, etc.)
- description of the metric
- actual result for that period
- goal or benchmark for that period
- desired trend (increasing positive? negative?)

Once you've input the data into your input template, you're ready to produce the outupt. Figure 56 shows an example of an output based on the template in Figure 55.

Figure 56: Dashboard Output Template

Actual Results	Mar. 31, 2006	Jun. 30, 2006	Sept. 30, 2006
Revenue Growth (Period over Period Sales)	75,000.00	50,000.00	120,000.00
Training Impact on Sales (Isolated and Adjusted Percent Linked to Training)	2.00%	1.00%	7.00%
Productivity Per Employee (Revenue/Employees)	600.00	500.00	1,300.00
Learning Effectiveness (Average Test Scores)	75	78	90
Time to Job Impact (% of Employees Applying Training in First 60 Days)	35.00%	37.00%	90.00%

Goals	Mar. 31, 2006	Jun. 30, 2006	Sept. 30, 2006
Revenue Growth (Period over Period Sales)	100,000.00	100,000.00	100,000.00
Training Impact on Sales (Isolated and Adjusted Percent Linked to Training)	5.00%	5.00%	5.00%
Productivity Per Employee (Revenue/Employees)	1,000.00	1,000.00	1,000.00
Learning Effectiveness (Average Test Scores)	85	85	85
Time to Job Impact (% of Employees Applying Training in First 60 Days)	70.00%	70.00%	70.00%

Legend - Actual Results

0.00	> = 10% positive variance from prior result
0.00	Between 10% positive variance and 10% negative variance from prior result
0.00	> = 10% negative variance from prior result

Source: KnowledgeAdvisors Metrics That Matter

Figure 56 automatically calculates the results, period by period, and will place a color-coding on them based on the variance to prior period and against goal. In this example, any positive variance over prior period or goal greater than 10% is green. Any negative variance over prior period or goal greater than 10% is red, and any variance less than 10% is yellow. The color-coding helps the executive to quickly scan the dashboard for problem areas.

Dashboards can be more visual, if preferred. Figure 57 shows an example of a more visual approach to an L&D dashboard.

Figure 57: Visual L&D Dashboard

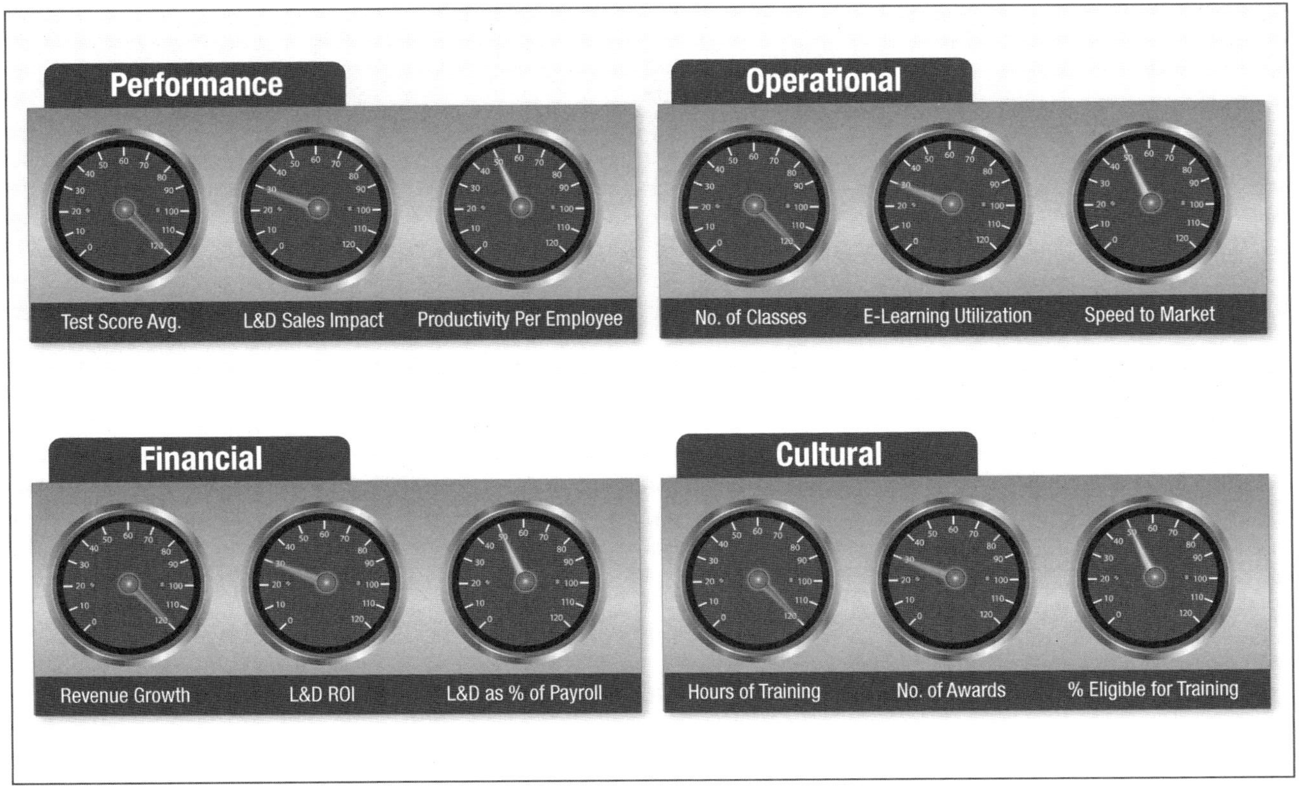

Performance

Test Score Avg. · L&D Sales Impact · Productivity Per Employee

Operational

No. of Classes · E-Learning Utilization · Speed to Market

Financial

Revenue Growth · L&D ROI · L&D as % of Payroll

Cultural

Hours of Training · No. of Awards · % Eligible for Training

Source: KnowledgeAdvisors

Figure 57 shows dials like a car instrument panel, and
the needles on the dial provide directional indicators.

Another approach to a basic scorecard or dashboard
is simply to use the evaluation data and put it on a
card each quarter. Figure 58 shows a sample
scorecard using follow-up data from a standard
follow-up evalution.

Figure 58: On-the-Job Performance Summary Scorecard

On-the-Job Performance Summary

	Metrics that Matter Benchmark	
	1/1 to 3/31	10/1 to 12/31
Respondents in Analysis	33,048	29,320
Performance Improvement	**High**	**High**
Definitely Applied Knowledge/Skills on Job	55.84%	59.40%
Experienced Significant On-the-Job Performance Improvements	37.80%	39.20%
Estimated Improvement in Performance Due to Training (adjusted for bias)	3.00%	3.00%
Results	**High**	**High**
Felt the Program had a Significant Impact on Increasing Quality	52.80%	53.30%
Felt the Program had a Significant Impact on Decreasing Costs	16.60%	14.50%
Felt the Program had a Significant Impact on Decreasing Cycle Time	31.80%	31.70%
Felt the Program had a Significant Impact on Increasing Productivity	53.40%	52.70%
Felt the Program had a Significant Impact on Increasing Sales	6.50%	5.20%
Felt the Program had a Significant Impact on Increasing Customer Satisfaction	32.10%	31.70%
Felt the Program had a Significant Impact on Increasing Employee Satisfaction	37.30%	34.20%
Value	**High**	**High**
Felt the Program was a Very Worthwhile Investment	59.30%	56.40%
Estimated Benefit to Cost Ratio from Training	1.5 to 1	1.5 to 1

Source: KnowledgeAdvisors Metrics That Matter

Figure 58 simply collects evaluation results in a practical way and puts them on a succinct card with business terminology.

KnowledgeAdvisors uses special scorecards for their own employee development and customer education programs. Figure 59 has a sample of the dashboards used by KnowledgeAdvisors to monitor learning effectiveness.

KnowledgeAdvisors Actual Results Scorecard

Time Period: January 1 - May 31, 2006

Query date: June 6

Actual Results	Jan-06	Feb-06	Mar-06	Apr-06
Productivity (Revenue per employee)	$14,536.46	$12,700.80	$14,510.80	$13,408.17
Revenue Growth (Period over period growth rate)		-8%	13%	-11%
Profitability (Human capital contribution margin)	38%	37%	34%	40%
Learning Activity (No. of learners completing training)	58	110	142	84
Investment (Actual L&D Expense)	$4,200.00	$2,700.00	$4,500.00	$4,500.00
Growth (No. of Reports Run)	43,781	49,331	52,950	52,265
Customer Loyalty (Client Retention Rate)		99%	100%	100%
Risk Mitigation (% of Dissatisfied Clients)	13%	5%	5%	8%
Actual Results Goals	**Jan-06**	**Feb-06**	**Mar-06**	**Apr-06**
Productivity (Revenue per employee)	$12,826.09	$13,260.87	$15,434.78	$13,854.17
Revenue Growth (Period over period growth rate)		3%	16%	-6%
Profitability (Human capital contribution margin)	29%	31%	41%	32%
Learning Activity (No. of learners completing training)	100	100	100	100
Investment (Actual L&D Expense)	$5,000.00	$5,000.00	$5,000.00	$5,000.00
Growth (No. of Reports Run)	43,000	44,720	46,508	48,369
Customer Loyalty (Client Retention Rate)		100%	100%	100%
Risk Mitigation (% of Dissatisfied Clients)	7%	7%	7%	7%

Source: KnowledgeAdvisors

Figure 59: KnowledgeAdvisors Scorecard (cont.)

If you feel you were successful in applying this learning please provide a few tangible examples of how you applied it.

I have been able to comfortably use the MTM system with very few problems.

Using MTM will enhance our ability to gather effective information from associates who attend our training classes. We will also be able to report back training information to business managers in a more effective way.

I will review the reports related to my courses and act to enhance my performance with successive classes. Comparing to benchmarks will allow me to add credibility to suggestions for improved courses in the future.

I will apply this training by providing Human Capital and Report Cards to each of our training units. I will also use it to identify courses that need improvement against the broad spectrum of all of our training. Finally, I will use it to tout our success by demonstrating it's results.

Course Types	No. of Evals	Satisfaction	Learning Effectiveness	Job Impact	Improvement %	ROI %
MTM Benchmark	731898	6.08	5.96	5.57	8.00%	400%
Our Goals		6.00	5.75	5.50	5.00%	350%
Our Average	228	5.80	5.67	5.50	3.52%	340%
Conferences and Events	35	5.72	4.70	5.28	3.28%	9%
Internal Development	17	6.68	6.18	6.69	7.38%	1376%
Learning Analytics	59	5.74	5.98	5.58	3.55%	245%
Metrics that Matter	93	5.63	5.55	5.60	2.69%	348%

Clients	No. of Evals	Overall	Job Impact	Business Results	Return on Investment
MTM Benchmark	796147	6.04	5.76	5.76	5.85
Our Goals		5.90	5.50	5.25	5.75
Our Average	245	5.70	5.63	4.96	5.54
Unassigned	170	5.76	5.67	5.01	5.61
ABN Amro	11	5.08	5.56	4.33	5.57
ADP	1	6.46	5.50	5.50	6.25
BT Learning	1	3.94	5.00	4.00	3.00
OAU	1	6.67	5.00	6.00	7.00

Source: KnowledgeAdvisors

Figure 59: KnowledgeAdvisors Scorecard (cont.)

Instructors	No. of Evals	% of 1-4	% of 6-7
MTM Benchmark	591618	4	82
Our Goals		5	75
Our Average	150	13	70
Berk, Jeffrey	51	20	60
Fuqua, Megan	16	1	85
Grisenthwaite, Jeff	13	0	87
Hahn, Alex	28	16	66
Mbah, Keiru	12	33	50
Rath, Amy	8	4	88
Trotter, Michelle	6	19	39
Voce, Samantha	7	0	90

Monthly Trend: Instructor Scale Average

Jan. 31, '06   Feb. 28, '06   Mar. 31, '06   Apr. 30, '06   May 31, '06

KnowledgeAdvisors Monthly Trends: Performance and Activity

Query date: June 6

Monthly Performance

Time Period: January 1 - May 31, 2006

Category	01-30-06	02-28-06	03-31-06	04-30-06	05-31-06
Business Results	4.97	5.50	4.92	4.66	5.00
Courseware	5.77	5.89	5.63	5.83	5.92
Environment	6.33	4.83		4.71	6.55
Instructor	5.83	6.04	5.85	6.03	6.09
Job Impact	5.65	5.93	5.57	5.37	5.62
Learning Effectiveness	5.33	6.14	5.88	5.37	5.80
Online Delivery	5.16	5.46	5.32	5.82	5.65
Return on Investment	5.35	6.00	5.55	5.52	5.67
Support Tools	4.25	4.19	4.50	5.30	4.47

Source: KnowledgeAdvisors

Figure 59 gives three views to the scorecard:

The first view focuses on results of the organization so that the executives responsible for learning can trend the organizational results.

The second view shows the major programs, instructors, and clients so that the learning executives can better understand the strategic learning elements and evaluate them.

The final view shows a trend analysis of the key performance indicators collected on evaluations so that the learning executives can monitor these over time and continue to improve.

A final thought on dashboards — automation. Many L&D managers feel that automation must happen in order for a dashboard or scorecard to exist. That is not true. You can create a nice template on a spreadsheet. You can key data into a template in that spreadsheet. Automation and linked systems make things easier, but not having them should not stop you from creating a dashboard. We suggest you begin by identifying your metrics, goals, and benchmarks, and collect the data manually a few quarters to make sure the data is what you would like before linking up systems, which may be a more challenging task.

X. Change Management in Analytics

A successful learning analytics program relies on the ability to make changes. An area where organizations are making dramatic changes is in the way they measure the impact of their learning investments. No longer are smile sheets at the end of class the norm. Organizations are linking training to business results, conducting deeper analysis, sending out supervisor and on-the-job surveys, and calculating financial returns. All of these changes need to be managed appropriately for maximum benefit. This chapter will discuss the change management ramifications when migrating to a new form of evaluation and measurement.

First, let's take a look at Figure 60, which shows the way in which humans react to change.

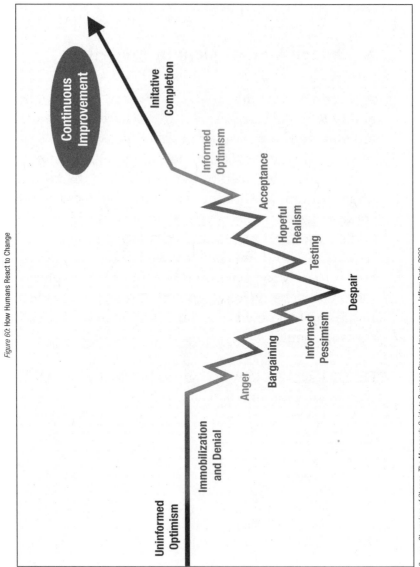

Figure 60: How Humans React to Change

Uninformed Optimism

Immobilization and Denial

Anger

Bargaining

Informed Pessimism

Despair

Testing

Hopeful Realism

Acceptance

Informed Optimism

Initative Completion

Continuous Improvement

Source: *Champions of Change, The Manager's Guide to Business Process Improvement*, Jeffrey Berk, 2003

Figure 60 shows that if we fail to anticipate change in our processes, we run a serious risk that the change will fail, not because of poor design but because of poor change management.

L&D managers should try to avoid reaching despair. How is this done? First, the leader of the change should be prepared to answer these questions in a clear and concise manner:

- What are we doing, and why?
- How does change relate to our objectives and strategies?
- Is management really committed?
- What is the change plan? Is it doable?

The major best practices that one should consider for successful change management for learning analytics include the following:

- Buy-in from management
- Overcoming the "old way" mentality
- Having an effective change agent
- Keeping the momentum alive

Our research shows what others have done to accomplish these practices.

The best way to get buy-in from management is to present a tangible list of benefits expected from this change. The most popular benefits communicated to management for buy-in include the following:

- Linkage to business results
- Increased quality of training
- Time savings in reporting results
- Practical ROI computations
- Better data for future decisions
- Increased customer satisfaction
- Reduced risk (defensible budget)

To overcome resistance and the old way of doing things, most organizations continue to emphasize benefits. They do this in the following ways:
- Communicate early and often
- Get buy-in from respected stakeholders
- Get quick wins to keep momentum
- Quantify results of future benefits

An effective change agent is a critical success factor. For organizations that have had an effective change agent, the major attributes of the change leader are the following:

- Communication skills
- People management skills
- Measurement skills
- Project management skills
- Political skills (within an organization)

In order to keep momentum alive, best practice organizations do the following to ensure success for learning analytics:

- Provide regular progress updates
- Publish the outputs of the analytics
- Continue to provide training and support

- Publish internal success stories
- Get the implementation done on time and on budget

Out of all that you can do to manage change for learning analytics, your number one effort should be to get those affected by the change involved early on. Seek their feedback and advice, but set expectations that not all they provide can be incorporated into the final decisions.

XI. Outsourcing Analytics Components

Outsourcing is the procuring of services or products, such as the parts used in manufacturing a motor vehicle, from an outside supplier or manufacturer in order to cut costs. In any outsourcing decision, including learning analytics, there are four crucial considerations before deciding on a full or partial outsource:

1. Time: Managing the things you don't have time to control
2. Resources: Keeping your team focused on needed tasks
3. Competency: Obtaining more effective from the experts
4. Economics: Weighing cost effectiveness vs. recruiting & hiring costs

So why consider outsourcing components of learning analytics specifically? Here are some of the most common reasons seen in the marketplace:

- Demonstrating learning value is a top priority.
- Few learning professionals have analytics experience.
- Many don't know where to begin, what to measure, how to measure it.
- Limited time, resources, budget.

Making an outsourcing decision involves other considerations in the process. These are as follows:

- *Planning*: Assess needs - Identify providers - Develop RFP
- *Selection*: Identify appropriate providers – Evaluate – Select provider
- *Management*: Manage relations - Measure performance

Specifically with learning analytics, there are three primary areas that should be considered for outsourcing. These are as follows, and each will be discussed in more detail:

- Strategy development
- Process development & deployment
- Analysis services

First, let's consider strategy. This is the documented plan to achieve your desired outcome. The major components in this area of learning analytics include the following:

- Measurement strategy — the actual writing of the strategy itself; the blueprint for the measurement process

- Readiness assessment — an upfront gap analysis to understand the difference between your current state and the desired state

- Evaluation instrument — the standard template(s) that will drive your process

- Architect the right technology solutions — understanding the technology requirements from both a technical and functional perspective

- Change of management strategy — tasks needed to ensure that the strategy and process succeed and that management and those affected by change are on board with the change

- Dashboard development and architecture — creation of the dashboard or scorecard macro and micro indicators and assignment of challenging yet attainable goals for each

All of the above are possible areas where a third-party consultant specializing in learning analytics can provide assistance and facilitate the process. The outsource provider may also offer a fresh perspective in these areas.

The second area for outsource consideration is process. This includes the resources, workflows, and tools to execute the strategy. Major components may include the following:

- Technology deployment — underlying technology necessary to collect, store, process, and report the data

- Systems integration — relationships between systems (HRIS to LMS, LMS to analytics)

- Systems administration — day-to-day use and maintenance of the systems and processes around the systems (e.g., scheduling of classes, manual input of paper data, sending of reminder messages)

The process area is probably the most outsourced. It is a composite of rote tasks that, once in place, need to be managed. Technology is the number one outsourced item, as it is far cheaper to buy it from a best practice company that focuses on it than to build and maintain custom software.

The third area for outsource consideration is analysis. Analysis is how you make sense of the data and communicate it to others. Below are some of the major considerations in analysis outsourcing:

- Quarterly and annual reports — preparation of higher level reports summarizing a milestone period

- Impact studies and ROI analysis — a deeper analysis of a strategic, visible, or costly program

- Data analysis from disparate sources — working from data that may be currently in multiple places (spreadsheets, paper, databases), experts can create a single repository for analysis

- Statistical analysis — analysis of data for statistical significance (ANOVA analysis, analysis of the means, etc.)

- Linking to business results — identifying actual results and providing a reasonable, credible link to them from the learning program

- Benchmark analysis — comparing organizational data to an external or internal set of comparable data to motivate by example

- Expert commentary — showcasing the most important observations as seen in the data and the most important opportunities for improvement

This area — analysis — is also a popular outsourced area. The main reason is third-party objectivity. Organizations may believe that their results will be tainted in management's eyes unless an independent third party performs the analysis.

Finally, when making outsourcing decisions consider the following business risks and develop controls to mitigate them:

- Liability and coverage issues
- Disaster recovery issues

- Ownership issues
- Fees, contract duration, reporting provisions
- Performance standards
- Procedures for changes and modifications
- Termination procedures

Outsourcing, if managed properly, can be an effective way to save money and get better end results. The entire analytics function need not be outsourced. However, a careful "make vs. buy" decision should be done prior to making internal investments in strategy, process, or analysis-related areas.

XII. Best Practices in Learning Analytics

This book has covered a variety of ways in which an organization can modify its existing analytics process. With a small amount of resources and with scalable approaches, you can create a more accountable measurement process.

To conclude, remember these important best practices for learning analytics, many of which were major themes of this book.

Best Practice #1: *Plan your metrics before writing survey questions.*

First and foremost, never ask a question on a data collection instrument unless it ties to a metric you will utilize. As simple as these sounds, organizations often create questions with no purpose in mind.

A great example is a consumer services company that invested enormous resources in custom surveys that were specific to each course with little or no comparability across courses. When asked if the value of collecting this data was beneficial to management, the company stated that while the data was great for course designers, it had gained little interest in the eyes of senior management or other stakeholders.

So, never write survey questions or collect data unless it results in a metric your stakeholders find valuable. Once you have finalized your set of metrics, the survey questions are an easy byproduct.

Best Practice #2: *Ensure that the measurement process is replicable and scalable.*

Organizations tend to spend thousands of dollars on one-off projects to measure a training program in detail. This information is collected over many months with exhaustive use of consultants and internal resources. Although the data are powerful and compelling, management often comes back with a response such as "Great work, now do the same thing for all the training." Unfortunately, such one-off measurement projects are rarely replicable on a large-scale basis. So don't box yourself into that corner.

A classic example is a telecommunications company that hired an expert third party to evaluate a single training program. The third party provided a convincing argument to management that the single program was a good use of company resources. Management quickly mandated that the same process be done for all programs. This was not feasible, given resource constraints. The training group had boxed themselves into a corner and was forced to quickly come up with a scaled-down process that could be replicated and scaled, yet they had to backtrack and resell the revised approach to management.

Make sure that you create a measurement process that can be replicated and scaled across all learning events without spending more on measurement than you do on training. To do this, you must acknowledge and accept that not everything needs in-depth, precise measures. The key is to use reasonable assumptions to predict and estimate learning effectiveness. Doing so will provide a baseline for you to manage by measurement and extract relevant data points to present to management that clearly demonstrate the value of the learning investments. This is not to rule out having the flexibility in your measurement process to drill deep into a program 5 to 10% of the time where it warrants such an exercise. You simply want to make sure that what you do 90 to 95% of the time is replicable and scalable.

Best Practice #3: *Ensure that measurements are internally and externally comparable.*

Related to Best Practice #2 is the concept of comparability. It is a significantly less powerful endeavor to do a one-off exercise when you have no baseline of comparability. If you spend several months calculating out a 300% ROI on your latest program, how do you know if that is good or bad? Surely, a 300% ROI is a positive return, but what if the average ROI on training programs is 1000%?

A great example is a manufacturer that believed they were an excellent training organization. Day in and day out they measured performance of instructors, courses, and facilities. The scores were always consistent. Finally, they compared against an external group of other organizations and found that they were consistently lower than other training organizations.

Ensuring that your measurement process is comparable both internally and externally is critical. Comparing learning effectiveness for each course, comparing investment value by each client grouping, or comparing job impact by key program are just a few examples of how internal and external comparisons can give you a more accurate portrayal of how your training is measuring up.

Best Practice #4: *Use industry-accepted measurement approaches.*

Management is looking to the training group to lead the way in training measurement. It is the job of the training group to convince management that their approach to measurement is reasonable. This is not unlike a finance department that must convince management of the way the department values assets.

In both cases, the group must ensure that the approach is based on industry-accepted principles that have proof of concept externally and merit internally.

A good example is a software company that was tasked with the challenge of determining a return on investment for their thousands of learning offerings. Senior management wanted to know the value of the training. The training group researched several methods and approaches, looking at books, articles, consultants, and associations such as the American Society for Training and Development. At the end of the day, the company adapted an approach that emphasized the models used by Donald Kirkpatrick in his Four Levels of Learning and Jack J. Phillips in his ROI Process. Senior management was able to more quickly buy into the approach, based on the overwhelming external support for these methodologies.

Regardless of the approach you use, keep in mind that you need to *adapt* it to your organization, not *adopt* it in your organization. There is a big difference. Adapting means taking an approach and tweaking it to fit your needs. It is not a cookie-cutter approach. Make sure you are comfortable with the approach and can defend it. Looking at its application by others and its acceptance in the industry will enable you to become more comfortable with the approach and make it more defensible when discussing it with management.

Best Practice #5: *Define value in the eyes of your stakeholders.*

If you ask people what they mean by "return on investment," you are likely to get more than one answer. In fact, odds are you'll get several. Return on investment is in the eyes of the beholder. To some, it could mean a quantitative number, and to others it could be a warm and fuzzy feeling.

For example, to showcase the diversity in value, let's look at two very different perspectives. A large utility defines value in measuring the financial, monetary return on every class they run. The value is in comparing the returns to each other and showcasing to management that the benefits exceed the costs of training. Contrast this to a very large oil company. This organization is far less concerned with a financial ROI on training. The company places enormous value on ensuring that the employees receive a quality training experience. The ROI for this company is the warm and fuzzy feeling they get when they review evaluations and know that the employee was satisfied with the training.

Had you calculated a financial ROI for the oil company, it might have been a waste of your time. However, if all you showed the utility were the "warm and fuzzies," they would have felt your measurement was not adequate. The point is to know your stakeholders. Understand how they define value. Ensure that your measurement process and your resulting metrics yield business intelligence that is of value to each stakeholder.

Best Practice #6: *Manage the change associated with measurement.*

As you can likely see, some of the best practices may be doomed for failure if you fail to manage the change with your stakeholders. Successful organizations will spend considerable time and energy planning for the change.

A best practice company is a large, international manufacturer. The corporate university rolled out a measurement process that would significantly change how the organization evaluates training. To manage this change, the organization slowly built it up during the implementation process. First, the leaders of the corporate university got the buy-in from stakeholders by getting them involved in the establishment of metrics and finalization of data collection instruments. Second, the corporate university sent out communications in its newsletters describing the timetables and benefits of the change. As a result, the organization fully embraced the new measurement process. In fact, the corporate university now receives measurement requests from conference planners and decentralized learning groups within the organization.

Any change must be managed. Failure to get buy-in from stakeholders can create hostility and resistance to change. Assess the culture and the readiness for change. Plan for change or plan to fail.

Best Practice #7: *Ensure that the metrics are well-balanced.*

Although you want to understand the needs of your stakeholders and have your stakeholders define how they perceive value, you also need to be proactive in ensuring that your final "measurement scorecard" is well balanced.

One IT organization was told that satisfaction was the sole measure of learning performance. This organization focused its efforts on measuring satisfaction across such items as instructor, courseware, and facility. It received excellent metrics on satisfaction. However, when it came time to answer the question regarding the impact of training on the job, or its return on investment, the organization did not have the data to support it. Too much emphasis was placed on one element of learning measurement.

A lopsided approach to measurement is risky. Using the popular Don Kirkpatrick model, you can see a balanced scorecard emerging from each of the four levels of learning he writes about. The first attribute is reaction. It is important to measure reaction, as that can help improve future events and is a proxy for satisfaction. The second attribute is learning. Just because people are happy does not mean they learned anything. It is critical to measure learning either through testing or through alternative predictors. The third attribute is behavior. If a person learned something, can you imply that that person changed his behavior on the job? Probably not. That is why you need to measure it. The final attribute is results. Did the training positively impact the business results as management felt it should have? As you can see, each level is like a quadrant in a scorecard. Some stakeholders may care more about certain quadrants than others, but the key is to keep the scorecard balanced so that you can comprehensively measure your investment, and continue to improve.

Best Practice #8: *Leverage automation and technology.*

Although this goes hand and hand with a measurement process that is replicable and scalable, it is worthy of separate mention. Your measurement process must leverage technology and automation to do the heavy lifting in areas such as data collection, storage, processing, and reporting.

A classic example is a mid-sized accounting firm. The company collected training surveys via paper and manually keyed them into an Excel spreadsheet. Requests for information often took hours to fulfill and could not be done in a timely manner.

In today's world of automation and technology, any company, large or small, can cost-effectively leverage technologies such as the Internet to collect data. Even when no computer is in the classroom, surveys can be e-mailed to participants after the training. With proper reinforcement a decent response rate can be gleaned. In addition, technologies for scanning paper data can avoid manual data entry. Finally, software technologies exist to create standardized reports using the collected data. The end result is that you spend fewer resources collecting, processing, and reporting results and more time analyzing the data for improvement purposes or for showcasing the value of the training back to management.

Best Practice #9: *Crawl, walk, run.*

When designing a learning measurement strategy, it pays to have a long-term vision, but don't attempt to put your entire vision in place right out of the blocks. The best approach is to start with the low-hanging fruit that can be done in a reasonable time frame to prove the concept, demonstrate a "win," and build a jumping-off point to the next level.

A great example is an insurance company that envisioned a measurement strategy that measured across a balanced scorecard of learning, leveraged automation, and provided relevant, timely metrics to key stakeholders. Recognizing the challenge of limited resources and lack of consistent technologies within the organization, this company started out by piloting the process on a few key programs. The pilots afforded the company the opportunity to test-drive the process, refine it, and build momentum for expanded usage. Now the company is rolling out the process organization-wide with the goal of integrating various systems involved in the process soon after.

Although it may be difficult for you, your first step should not be a step at all but rather a crawl. You can learn a lot from a pilot or test-run of your process. Also, you build the quick wins you need to sustain momentum to move the process forward in the organization.

Best Practice #10: *Ensure that your metrics have flexibility.*

The last thing you want to do is roll out a measurement process that is inflexible. You will likely have people who want to view the same data but in many different ways. You need to have architected your database to accommodate this important issue, thereby creating measurement flexibility.

For example, a large technology training company has multiple stakeholders who want to see the same data from different perspectives because they manage different aspects of the business. The courseware designers need to see the training data sliced by course in order to understand which courses generate the greatest job impact. The team that manages instructors needs to slice the data by instructor in order to monitor the quality levels of their large group of professional instructors. Senior management wants to view the data by location. Each location is in effect a separate entity, and the performance and quality levels of each is of keen importance to them. Finally, the sales and marketing folks want to mine the data for intelligence surrounding historical performance and productivity gains experienced by learners as a result of the training. This helps them create better business cases when positioning the training to prospective buyers.

As can be seen by the above example, you need to carefully think about the data before you collect them. Once the data is collected, you are limited with what you got. The saying "garbage in is garbage out" is true. Most commonly, you should want to "tag" every data element with the following: instructor name (if applicable), learning delivery mode, location of training, learning provider (internal or external), date of training, course name, curricula (group the course belongs to), and program (group the curricula belong to). To make matters easier, technologies such as OLAP cubes can be used to slice this data in near infinite proportions, satisfying the needs of all of your data requests.

Finally, flexibility is inherent in your ability to "roll up" the data. This, too, must be considered prior to data collection. Often, companies ask different questions for each course. That is good tactical detail but not good strategic intelligence. Different data is more challenging to aggregate up into higher levels. Senior management is far more likely to want to view aggregate data than class- or course-specific data. So, ensure that you have a common set of "standard" questions that can be asked across all courses and aggregated and benchmarked. You can still have course-specific questions for the more tactical analysis. In this way you have more flexibility in your data.

Edward Hubbard, PhD, consultant and author, once said, "Training is either at the table working with senior management and adding value or they are on the table perceived as a cost center that is going to get cut." The best practices mentioned are not an all-inclusive list of what it takes to avoid being on the table. However, they should serve as a sobering reminder to us all that not even the biggest and best training organizations are protected against the reality or perception that one's value can come into question at any time. Leverage the practices and be a step ahead by creating the right measurement approaches to continuously improve and showcase value to stakeholders.

About the Authors

Kent D. Barnett
Founder and CEO, KnowledgeAdvisors, Inc.

Kent started KnowledgeAdvisors in 2000 with the goal of helping organizations measure and improve the impact of people. Since that time, Kent and his talented team from KnowledgeAdvisors have worked with hundreds of leading organizations around the world to develop best practices in this area. KnowledgeAdvisors is now the clear market leader in learning and development measurement.

Prior to 2000, Kent was a corporate banker and president of a major technology training company. As a banker, Kent learned to help organizations maximize shareholder value through ROI analysis, including returns on human capital investments. As the president of a global training company, Kent used his financial analysis skills to create measurable value for corporate clients.

He has an MBA in finance from Northwestern University's Kellogg School of Management. Kent is certified in the Stern Stewart Economic Value Added (EVA) Methodology.

Jeffrey A. Berk
Chief Operating Officer, KnowledgeAdvisors, Inc.

Jeffrey joined KnowledgeAdvisors in 2001. He works closely with clients to implement the Metrics That

Matter® technology developed by
KnowledgeAdvisors and to devise appropriate
human capital and learning measurement strategies.

Prior to joining KnowledgeAdvisors, Jeffrey worked
with Andersen for nearly a decade. While with
Andersen he was the manager of benchmarking
services. He led the quantitative and qualitative
benchmarking initiatives on a global scale for the
firm.

Jeffrey is an adjunct professor of management at
Northwestern's Kellogg School of Management and
at Loyola University in the MBA program where he
teaches a course on performance improvement. He is
also an adjunct faculty member at DePaul University
where he teaches a class on learning evaluation. He is
the author of the book *Champions of Change: The
Manager's Guide to Sustainable Process Improvement.*

Jeffrey, a CPA, began his professional career as an
auditor before moving to consulting at Andersen and
then to KnowledgeAdvisors. He has an MBA from
the University of Chicago and degrees in business
and accounting from the University of Kansas.

About KnowledgeAdvisors

KnowledgeAdvisors is a human capital analytics firm. Its technology, Metrics That Matter, and complementary solutions provide a practical, scalable, and repeatable approach to measuring and analyzing learning programs and other talent management initiatives.

Using its Web-based evaluation system, Metrics That Matter, and its extensive database of performance benchmarks, KnowledgeAdvisors helps corporate universities, talent management departments, training companies, and other organizations measure and improve performance.

Footnotes:

I. Why Analyze Human Capital
   1. Becker, Gary, S., *Human Capital, A Theoretical and Empirical Analysis with Special Reference to Education*, 3rd edition, University of Chicago Press, 1992
   2. KnowledgeAdvisors Learning Analytics Best Practices Research Study, 2004
   3. Jack J. Phillips, *Return on Investment in Training and Performance Improvement Programs*, Gulf Publishing, Houston, Texas, 1997

II. Business Case for Measurement
   1. "Pulse Check," *T&D Magazine*, January 2006
   2. "The CLO Path," *T&D Magazine*, February 2006
   3. "GAO's Name Change and Other Provisions of the GAO Human Capital Reform Act of 2004," http://www.gao.gov/about/namechange.html

III. Identifying Human Capital Processes
   1. Bassi, Lauri, The Impact of U.S. Firm's Investments in Human Capital on Stock Prices, Bassi Investments, Inc., June 2004
   2. Becker, Gary, S., Human Capital: A Theoretical and Empirical Analysis with Special Reference to Education, 3rd Edition, University of Chicago Press, 1993
   3. Berk, Jeffrey A, Champions of Change: The Manager's Guide to Creating Sustainable Business Process Improvements, Word Association Publishers, Tarentum, PA, 2003

4. Fitz-enz, Jac, <u>ROI of Human Capital: Measuring the Economic Value of Employee Performance</u>, Amacom Books, New York, NY, 2000

5. Fitz-enz, Jac, <u>Workforce Intelligence Report</u>, Workforce Intelligence Institute, San Jose, CA, 2006

6. KnowledgeAdvisors, <u>Human Capital Contribution Model: A Systematic Approach for Learning Organizations to Assess Needs, Effectiveness, Business Results, ROI and Profit Impact</u>, 2005

7. Phillips, Jack, Phillips, Patti, Stone, Ron, <u>The Human Resources Scorecard: A Step-by-Step Guide for Measuring the Impact of Human Resources with Detailed Case Studies</u>, Butterworth Heinemann, Woburn, MA, 2001

8. PricewaterhouseCoopers, *Global Best Practices*, Universal Process Classification Scheme (www.globalbestpractices.com)

IV. Current Trends in Learning Measurement

1. "Training Analytics: What Works," Bersin & Associates, 2005

2. "Training Analytics: Market Research," Bersin & Associates, 2006

3. KnowledgeAdvisors Learning Analytics Best Practices Research Study, 2004

4. Bassi Investment Strategy, http://www.bassi-investments.com

5. KnowledgeAdvisors Learning Analytics Workshop, 2005

6. Becker, Gary S., *Human Capital, A Theoretical and Empirical Analysis with Special Reference to Education*, 3rd edition, University of Chicago Press, 1992

V. Human Capital Contribution Model
1. KnowledgeAdvisors, *Human Capital Contribution Model: A Systematic Approach for Learning Organizations to Assess Needs, Effectiveness, Business Results, ROI and Profit Impact*, 2005
2. KnowledgeAdvisors, Metrics That Matter Learning Analytics Technology, 2005
3. Jack J. Phillips, *Return on Investment in Training and Performance Improvement Programs*, Gulf Publishing, Houston, Texas, 1997
4. KnowledgeAdvisors, *Training Operations Best Practices Corporate Universities*, 2005

VI. Overview of Learning Analytics and Measurement Models
1. Jack J. Phillips, *Return on Investment in Training and Performance Improvement Programs*, Gulf Publishing, Houston, Texas, 1997
2. Kirkpatrick, Donald, *Evaluating Training Programs: The Four Levels*, 2nd Edition, Berrett-Koehler Publishers, Inc., San Francisco, 1998
3. KnowledgeAdvisors Response Rates Research Study, 2005

VII. Present Measurement Method that Is Practical
and Scalable
1. KnowledgeAdvisors, Metrics That Matter
   Learning Analytics Technology, 2005
2. KnowledgeAdvisors MTM Integration
   Overview, 2006
3. KnowledgeAdvisors Post-Event Survey, 2003

VIII. Valuation Models for Deriving Impact, Results
and ROI
1. KnowledgeAdvisors, Metrics That Matter
   Learning Analytics Technology, 2005
2. Jack & Patti Phillips Case Studies, courtesy of
   ROI Institute, 2004
3. KnowledgeAdvisors ROI Models white paper,
   2004
4. Appendix Case Study Courtesy of Kirk Smith,
   independent consultant, Raleigh, North
   Carolina

IX. Key Performance Indicators and Dashboards
1. KnowledgeAdvisors, Metrics That Matter
   Learning Analytics Technology, 2006
2. Corporate Executive Board, Profiles for L&D
   Dashboards, 2005
3. Charles Knight Presentation at Chicago-land
   Learning Leaders Conference, October 10, 2006

X. Change Management in Analytics
1. *Change Management Best Practices*,
   KnowledgeAdvisors, 2004

2. Berk, Jeffrey, *Champions of Change: The Manager's Guide to Business Process Improvement*, Word Association Publishers, Tarentum, PA, 2003

XI. Outsourcing Components of Learning Analytics
   1. *The American Heritage® Dictionary of the English Language*, 4th edition
   2. KnowledgeAdvisors, About Outsourcing presentation

XII. Best Practices in Learning Analytics
   1. Berk, Jeffrey, "Best Practices in Learning Measurement," *CLO Magazine*, October 2003